9.99

History

...UGHES and
KATH COX

Teacher Timesavers

Published by Scholastic Publications Ltd,
Villiers House,
Clarendon Avenue,
Leamington Spa,
Warwickshire CV32 5PR

© 1992 Scholastic Publications Ltd
Reprinted 1993
Revised edition 1995

Authors Pat Hughes and Kath Cox
Editor Magdalena Hernas
Sub-editor Jo Saxelby
Series designer Joy White
Designers Clare Brewer and Anna Oliwa
Illustrations Jane Bottomley
Cover illustration Frances Lloyd
Cover photograph Martyn Chillmaid

Artwork by Salvo Print, Leamington Spa
Printed in England by Clays Ltd, St Ives plc

British Library Cataloguing-in-Publication Data
A catalogue record for this book is available from the British Library.

ISBN 0-590-53485-8 2nd edition
(ISBN 0-590-53037-2 1st edition)

All rights reserved. This book is sold subject to the condition that it shall not, by way of trade or otherwise, be lent, hired out or otherwise circulated without the publisher's prior consent in any form of binding or cover other than that in which it is published and without a similar condition, including this condition, being imposed upon the subsequent purchaser.

No part of this publication may be reproduced, stored in a retrieval system, or transmitted, in any form or by any means, electronic, mechanical, photocopying, recording or otherwise, without the prior permission of the publisher. This book remains copyright, although permission is granted to copy pages 13 to 144 for classroom distribution and use only in the school which has purchased the book.

Acknowledgements
Text: p.77 transcription of inventory used by permission of J.E. Hollishead, Liverpool Institute of Higher Education; p.99 extract from 'Evidence from R.H., captain of Auschwitz' in **Skills in History: the twentieth century** by P. Shuter, T.C. Lewis and J. Child, reprinted by permission of Heinemann Publishers (Oxford); p.101 extract from **Testament of Experience** by Vera Brittain, reprinted by permission of Virago Press; p.104 extract from **War Boy** by Michael Foreman, reprinted by permission of Pavilion Books.
Illustrations: p.103 Crown copyright, the Imperial War Museum; p.125 reproduced courtesy of Mary Evans Picture Library; Illustrator's reference materials courtesy of: pp.33 and 50 'Bygones', Fore Street, St Marychurch, Torquay; p.39 Museum of Childhood, Beaumaris; p.59 Blackpool Tourist Information Office; p.60 the Post Office.

Contents

Teachers' notes   5

Key Stage 1

All about me
My life so far   13
My family   14
My favourite things   15
A family tree   16
A generation circle   17
The generation game   18
My patchwork quilt of memories   19
Childhood memories   20

People
People in school   21
People in fairy tales   22
People in legends   23
The Royal Family   24
The story of St Patrick   25
Harriet Tubman: a legend in her time   26
Famous nurses   27
Famous children   28

Places
Name the buildings   29
What has changed?   30
In the bedroom: then and now   31
In the street: then and now   32
At the shops: then and now   33
A homes time-line (1)   34
A homes time-line (2)   35
Famous places: where are they?   36

Celebrations
What does your family celebrate?   37
Christmas   38
Birthday celebrations   39
Birthday greetings   40
Special occasions   41
Matching artefacts   42
A spring myth   43
Easter eggs   44

Fun and games
My favourite toys   45
Toys: then and now   46
Children's books: then and now   47
Playing outside: then and now   48
Playground rhymes   49
A toyshop in the past   50
Make a doll time-line   51
Make a games time-line   52

Travel
Going places   53
Going to school: then and now   54
A pram time-line   55
In the Transport Museum   56
Famous travellers   57
Road transport time-line   58
Going to the seaside   59
Street furniture   60

Key Stage 2

Romans, Anglo-Saxons and Vikings in Britain
Planning grid   61
Britain   62
Britain before the Romans   63
Why bother with Britain?   64
A Roman town   65
An Anglo-Saxon village   66
A Viking town   67
What's in a name?   68
The 'three Rs' Roman style   69
Monks and manuscripts   70
Writing in runes   71
Invasion time-line   72

Life in Tudor times
Planning grid   73
Monarchs: the two Elizabeths   74
The Tudor family tree   75
The *Golden Hind*   76

Inventories	77
Women in Tudor times	78
Breakfast with Queen Elizabeth I	79
A Tudor kitchen	80
Religion in Tudor times	81
Elizabeth's advice to Mary Queen of Scots	82
A Tudor house	83
Who's who in Tudor times?	84

Victorian Britain

Planning grid	85
Victorian time-line	86
Victorian families	87
Court dwellings	88
Home sweet home	89
Victorian holidays	90
Children at work	91
Workhouse children	92
Victorian women	93
King Cholera	94
Inventions of the Victorian era	95
Famous Victorians	96

Britain since 1930

Planning grid	97
Key events time-line	98
The Holocaust	99
Nazi education	100
The Blitz	101
Evacuation	102
Wartime persuasion: evacuation	103
Staying at home	104
Identity cards for the under-sixteens	105
Rationing	106
The armed forces	107
At sea	108

Ancient Greece

Planning grid	109
Greece today	110
The Greek world of myths and legends	111
Mapping the Ancient Greek world	112
A time-ribbon of key events	113
Famous Greeks	114
The 1992 Olympic Games	115
Vase paintings	116
Evidence from Ancient Greece	117
Ships and shipping	118
The Greek alphabet	119
Technology problem from Ancient Greece	120

A past non-European society – The Aztecs

Planning grid	121
The world in 1450	122
Exploration time-line	123
Columbus and his crew	124
The Old World meets the New	125
Aztec life	126
Aztec men at work	127
Clues from the ground	128
Aztec writing	129
Aztec gods	130
The defeat of the Aztecs	131
The effects of exploration	132

Support materials

Teacher planning grid	133
Pupil record sheet	134
Resource evaluation: teacher's sheet (1)	135
Resource evaluation: teacher's sheet (2)	136
Pupil ideas sheet	137
Pupil comment sheet	138
History detectives: using evidence	139
Investigating an artefact	140
Our class museum	141
Time-line	142
Time-ribbon	143
Interview schedule	144

Teachers' Notes

Introduction
This book contains 132 photocopiable sheets designed to help teachers implement the requirements for history in the National Curriculum. It is not intended as a course in itself, but as additional classroom resource material. The ideas contained in the photocopiable sheets owe much to the primary teachers, students and children with whom we work and we are grateful to all of them for their help.

Introducing historical methodology

A sense of time
Time, or chronology in this context, is a vital element in history teaching. Sequencing activities and the creation of time-lines are key factors in promoting a sense of time. Early sequencing activities include:
- re-telling stories;
- recalling activities that have taken place, both inside and outside school;
- following a series of instructions;
- ordering materials such as artefacts and sequencing cards;
- recording days of the week, months and seasons of the year.

Early time-lines should be child-based, for example, a current photograph placed alongside one taken some time ago. A sense of time is most clearly understood when it utilises the child's own experiences and builds on them. These early, personal time-lines can gradually be built up during Key Stage 1, so that by the time children enter Key Stage 2 they have a clear sense of time in relation to their own lives and to the life of a known adult, such as a parent, carer or teacher.

At Key Stage 2, there are a wide variety of time-line activities. Each of the study units requires its own time-line. Whether this is placed within a more extensive time-line will depend on the age and ability of the children involved. Children learning about Romans, Anglo-Saxons or Vikings in Year 3 obviously require a different form of time-line from children covering the same theme in Year 6. Many children have real difficulties with chronology and even at the end of Key Stage 2 may still be limited to a 'now and then' approach.

A sense of place
History teaching often involves understanding about places. For example, when studying the Anglo-Saxons children need to look at maps which show where they came from. The maps themselves provide an historical source for explaining why people left their own homes to sail into the unknown. Several of the photocopiable pages in this book provide children with an opportunity to develop their awareness of maps as a key historical source. Maps of the UK are also important, as there is a tendency to assume that everything happened in and around the capital.

At both key stages, historical sources include the following:
- artefacts;
- pictures and photographs;
- adults talking about their own pasts;
- written sources;
- buildings and sites.

At Key Stage 2, teachers are required to introduce children to the features characteristic of the particular periods and societies studied and to be aware of the diversity that exists in the following aspects:
- social;
- cultural;
- religious;
- ethnic.

The content outlines for each study unit ensure that these aspects are built into every unit.

Using available evidence
Ideally, children should be presented with a variety of primary sources of historical evidence as they will need to learn how to interpret them. Some children will have problems in understanding, as well as interpreting, evidence which may be difficult to read or uses unfamiliar words. All children will need to consider the purposes and prejudices of both primary and secondary sources. Primary sources are original materials from the period and are just as liable to bias as secondary sources, which are gleaned from primary ones. Textbooks are the most obvious examples of secondary sources, although they may contain primary sources such as photographs.

It is important that children learn to use primary sources, both written and visual. Thus, in this book there is a great deal of primary source material, both as excerpts from documents and as illustrations, to give a wide range of interpretations and perspectives on historical events.

Change and continuity
Each historical period studied needs to be seen as part of a story which includes change and continuity. Children find change easier to interpret than continuity; the differences between 'now' and 'then' are often easier to find than the similarities. As the children move through the key stages, their skills should develop so that they perceive relationships between the past and the present.

The photocopiable sheets
The book is divided into three sections, the first containing Key Stage 1 activities, the second Key Stage 2 activities and the third a collection of general support material.

The Key Stage 1 section consists of six themes suggested in the original non-statutory guidance, each developed into eight photocopiable pages. These provide a means of recording children's understanding and should be seen as a supplement rather than a core activity.

To avoid the assumption that all children live in a particular type of family, many of the activities suggest that children ask an older person about his or her experiences. Where the issue of family relationships is a particularly sensitive one, then the Royal Family can be discussed instead.

The Key Stage 2 section is organised into six study units, each containing eleven photocopiable pages receded by a planning grid. The grids have been adapted from those given in the original non-statutory guidance – they reflect the authors' own teaching experiences and should be adapted for other children to reflect their interests and needs.

Some of the Key Stage 2 activities involve completing a time-line or time-ribbon to help children grasp the concept of chronology. These raise several issues about which events to include and should be used with care. Traditional history curriculum content has often been very narrow and commercial time-lines have tended to reflect this.

Several photocopiable pages require children to have access to reference material. These, together with the extension activities on most pages in this section, will enable children to use their higher-order reading and referencing skills.

Key Stage 1
All about me

My life so far The children should find out basic facts about themselves and add a picture of themselves to their sheet.

My family The layout is open-ended so that the children can use the sheet whatever their family situations. Follow-up questions could include the relative ages of family members such as older, younger, eldest, youngest.

My favourite things The focus here is on change and continuity in the types of food and clothing at different stages in the children's own lives. They can use catalogue pictures, draw or write their responses.

A family tree Again, the format is open-ended as it may not be appropriate to ask the children about their own families. Alternative suggestions are the Royal Family tree, a tree for a family in a story or the teacher's family tree.

A generation circle This is a more flexible alternative to the traditional family tree. The children draw portraits of the people they wish to include in the appropriate part of the circle and write their names in the spaces provided.

The generation game This activity asks the children to match the object to the person who might use it. It provides an opportunity to discuss gender stereotypes, for example, 'Do all grandmothers knit?' Items such as a newspaper could be matched to more than one person.

My patchwork quilt of memories This sheet is inspired by the story *The Patchwork Quilt* by V. Flournoy (1987) Picture Puffin. The time-scale for the activity has been restricted as children's sense of time is limited at this stage. Where appropriate, teachers will be able to extend the quilt of memories.

Childhood memories This simple questionnaire can be used by pupils to interview people about a range of topics. For example, an older child, a parent helper, the headteacher and an elderly person could be asked about their childhood memories of favourite toys.

People

People in school The children should use observation skills to describe the picture of a turn-of-the-century classroom before drawing a picture of their own. They can then compare the two, identifying similarities and differences.

People in fairy tales Children need to understand the difference between real people and fictional characters. The illustrations show three fairy-tale characters – the Sleeping Beauty, Cinderella and Dick Whittington – of whom the last is based on a real person. Discuss evidence that he really lived.

People in legends Legends are generally based on some historical fact, as are those about Queen Esther, Arthur and Robin Hood. Children should hear the stories and have access to visual material related to the relevant periods.

The Royal Family This sheet focuses on people who are both real and familiar. Newspapers and magazines will provide the necessary pictures. Discuss generations and relationships. Terms such as queen and princess can be explored in a modern context and compared to the fairy-tale stereotypes.

The story of St Patrick The children need to match sentences and pictures before they order the pictures and tell the story. Ask the children whether they think this is a true story or not and to explain their reasoning.

Harriet Tubman: a legend in her time This activity tells the story of Harriet Tubman, a 19c black American, born in slavery, who escaped and then helped other slaves to escape.

Famous nurses This activity requires the children to carry out simple research. You will need to provide appropriate material about Mary Seacole, Florence Nightingale, Edith Cavell and other famous nurses.

Famous children You will need reference material to support the children's research. You could suggest other famous children to be researched, eg the last Chinese Emperor or a contemporary teenage pop star.

Places

Name the buildings This activity involves the children in identifying four buildings. It may be used at the start of a topic to assess the children's knowledge and understanding – how do they know, for example, that the first building is a church? Can they identify characteristic features? Related fieldwork in the locality should accompany this activity.

What has changed? The children use their observation skills to identify changes made to a building over time. They should suggest reasons for the changes, for example, the removal of the chimneys reflects a change from coal fires to gas or electric heating.

In the bedroom: then and now Let the children observe and discuss what is in the picture and understand the functions of items such as the chamber pot. They can then draw a picture of a contemporary bedroom and explore the similarities and differences between the two.

In the street: then and now Let the children study the two pictures and discuss similarities and differences. Elements of change and continuity can be drawn out in the matching activity. For example, each street has lighting but the design and method have changed.

At the shops: then and now After comparing a Victorian shop with a modern supermarket, the children can explore the effects of the changes.

A homes time-line (1) The illustrations are a 13c castle, a Victorian back-to-back house and a modern semi. Ask the children to observe and discuss the pictures before placing them in the correct order, giving their reasons for doing so. Points of similarity and difference should be found. For example, all the homes have windows. Why is this? How have the windows changed? This activity can be extended by using it together with the next one.

A homes time-line (2) The illustrations show a 16c Tudor house, a cave and a 9c Viking house. This activity can be used on its own or in conjunction with the previous one to make an extended time-line.

Famous places: where are they? The original non-statutory guidelines for KS1 suggested extending children's knowledge of places through investigation of famous sites. This activity can be used in conjunction with a simple atlas and travel brochures of the countries concerned.

Celebrations

What does your family celebrate? This activity focuses on the children's own experiences of celebrations. The open-ended format allows them to consider a wide range of celebrations, noting the similarities such as cards and special foods. As a follow-up, discuss why we celebrate certain events.

Christmas The children are asked to identify the main reason for celebrating Christmas – the birth of Jesus Christ – as well as to draw or write about familiar aspects of Christmas.

Birthday celebrations The children should look carefully at the illustration and discuss what is happening before drawing their own picture. Questions such as, 'How do we know this is a party in the past?' help focus attention on detail.

Birthday greetings Let the children talk about the Victorian card. They can then draw a modern card. Follow-up discussion can focus on similarities and differences between the two.

Special occasions Many special events are celebrated with commemorative objects. Some children will have access to such objects, for example, christening plates or 21st birthday tankards. They could also look at objects celebrating 'Royal' events such as the mug shown here. The children should use the objects as sources of information. Why are certain events commemorated in this way?

Matching artefacts The children should match the artefact to the correct word and describe the Diwali celebration. Many will be able to draw on their own experiences; others will need more preliminary work. Links can be made with other celebrations, for example, fireworks are also used on Bonfire Night and during the Chinese New Year.

A spring myth The illustrations and sentences tell part of the Greek myth of Persephone. The story gives one explanation of the coming of spring. Tell the children the story and display pictures of life in Ancient Greece.

Easter eggs Spring and Easter celebrations feature traditionally decorated eggs as symbols of new life. Provide pictures of decorated eggs to help children compete the sheet. Extension work could focus on local Easter traditions.

Fun and games

My favourite toys This activity focuses on the key concepts of change and continuity as children identify the different types of toys that they have played with at various stages in their development. They can use catalogue pictures, draw or write their responses. This activity could be extended to consider older children.

Toys: then and now The children should draw their own favourite toy and then ask an older person about his or her favourite childhood toy. This will create an opportunity to discuss similarities and differences between toys now and some years ago.

Children's books: then and now This activity focuses on the key concepts of change and continuity through a comparison of styles of illustration in children's books. The children will draw their own version of a contemporary illustration and compare it with the example of a typical 1930s illustration.

Playing outside: then and now The illustration shows Victorian children playing marbles and skipping, both of which are still played today. Ask the children to draw examples of outdoor games they play and to talk about the differences and similarities.

Playground rhymes Playground rhymes have almost disappeared in many areas and there children will need to learn some, perhaps by asking older people who remember their childhood rhymes, before they complete the sheet.

A toyshop in the past This activity asks the children to identify anachronistic items. It can be used at the start of a topic on 'Toys' to assess the level of understanding and/or at the end. It is important that the children are asked to give reasons for their answers. Some will only be able to identify the items that are wrong, others will give the right answer for the wrong reason.

Make a doll time-line This activity focuses on sequencing and the language of chronology, for example, older than, oldest, newest, before, after. Initial discussion is essential to help the children look for clues that will help them work out the correct order for the pictures before making their time-lines. The examples shown are a jointed, Roman doll (bottom right); a Tudor doll (top left); a Victorian doll (bottom left), and a modern one (top right).

Make a games time-line This activity looks at similarities and differences, as well as elements of change and continuity. Discuss the pictures and look for clues to put them in the right order. Draw attention to appearance and dress. The examples shown are Viking children skating (bottom right); a Roman hoop game (top right); Tudor children playing with a hobby-horse (bottom left), and modern children on skateboards (top left).

Travel

Going places This activity begins with the children's own experiences of travel as babies, toddlers and now. They can discuss why different transport is appropriate at different stages of development.

Going to school: then and now After identifying their own experiences, the children should interview older people about their memories of going to school (oral history), comparing the experiences and identifying similarities and differences. In follow-up discussion, consider why fewer children walk to school now or why older people had to walk long distances.

A pram time-line The children should look at the pictures of prams (Victorian, modern and 1930s) and describe what they see, and then sequence them with the oldest first and the newest last. They should explain their ordering and identify similarities and differences in style, materials and so on.

In the Transport Museum The children should identify means of transport from the past. They will need pictures and reference books for their research. Ask them to compare and contrast the old with the new, for example, a modern train with a Stephenson's Rocket.

Famous travellers The children will need access to a globe to complete this sheet. Atlases, travel brochures and books will also be useful. Mary Kingsley is selected as only one of a group of intrepid women travellers – unfortunately, many books give the impression that men did all the travelling. The children can use reference books to find out more about the times in which these individuals lived.

Road transport time-line The illustrations show road transport through time (from top left, clockwise); a Roman litter, an 18c stage-coach, a Benz car (the first motor car), a Victorian hansom cab, a modern car and a 15c cart. The children should have time to observe and discuss these pictures and familiarise themselves with the new vocabulary. Once they have placed the pictures in the correct order, from oldest to newest, they should explain their reasons for the order. Draw out elements of continuity and change.

Going to the seaside The two illustrations show Blackpool at the turn of the century and today. The children should compare the means of transport, seaside activities, clothing, etc, and note similarities and differences. For example, the tram is a good example of continuity.

Street furniture This activity focuses on one type of street furniture which should be familiar to all children. The illustrations show examples of post-boxes from the Victorian period and the reign of George V. The children can compare the two before drawing a modern example. (Fieldwork will be needed here.)

Key Stage 2
Romans, Anglo-Saxons and Vikings in Britain

General The children should receive a brief overview of the three periods of invasion and settlement before focusing on a particular one. The concept of invasion is difficult – perhaps you could arrange for a colleague, preferably from another school, to 'invade' your class and turn the children out of their classroom for the day. The emphasis in these activities is on settlement rather than invasion as this topic can be presented all too easily as a succession of pillaging soldiers!

Planning grid This discusses the inhabitants of Britain before the Roman invasion. In areas where there are local resources for the Iron Age this aspect could be covered in greater detail and linked to a local study unit. The choice of a later settlement for an in-depth study should also be guided by local considerations such as available museums.

Britain This blank map can be used to plot key Roman towns, roads and forts, as well as the patterns of the different settlements through place-names (see 'What's in a name?', page 68).

Britain before the Romans It is important for the children to realise that Britain was not an empty space awaiting invasion. The map enables them to identify the Celtic tribes that lived in the area and provides a context for finding out about the Celts. If local sources are readily available, more time could be spent on looking at the cultures of pre-Roman Britain.

Why bother with Britain? This activity directs the children to relate the Roman Empire to modern European countries and to consider the reasons for invasion (to secure the defence of the empire as a result of tribal disputes in Britain and raids on Roman-held France; to acquire Britain's natural resources and increase trade; to uphold the glory of Rome and increase the prestige of Emperor Claudius).

A Roman town This activity focuses on the settlement aspect of the invasion. Roman towns acted as centres of trade, law and order. They also provided a showcase for Roman life and civilisation, encouraging the population to adopt Roman ways. Viroconium (Wroxeter) was a carefully planned town with a city hall, market, shops, baths, an underground water supply and a sewerage system.

An Anglo-Saxon village The Saxons were village dwellers rather than townspeople. The picture shows a typical 'tun' – a defended village. The fence kept out raiders and wolves. Typical village sites included river crossings, natural harbours, good grazing land, areas rich in mineral or clay deposits. Comparisons can be made with the Roman town on page 65.

A Viking town The focus here is on the settlement aspect of the Viking invasions. The picture shows a typical Viking town. Although many Vikings settled on farms, their interest in trade and crafts resulted in the establishment of many towns. Comparisons could be made with the Roman town on page 65 and the Anglo-Saxon village on page 66.

What's in a name? This activity enables the children to establish the patterns of settlement and to make links between past and present through an investigation of place-names.

The 'three Rs' Roman style Through this activity the children will see how elements of the Roman language and number systems are still in use today. Museums may provide 'hands on' experience of the Roman writing implements. *Bright Ideas History* by Lucy Hall (1987) Scholastic, gives instructions for making a wax tablet. For some pupils, you could introduce dictionary work to find words of Latin origin. Examples of Roman numerals still in use include clocks, watches, book chapters, BBC television credits (date).

Monks and manuscripts The Anglo-Saxons used runes for writing. This illuminated style is associated with the spread of Christianity. Monks wrote with a stylus on vellum made from animal skins. Ideally, the children should have access to more examples of calligraphy and illumination in order to appreciate the intricate designs and to help them with their own.

Writing in runes Runic alphabets vary in the number of letters. Most surviving runic inscriptions are to do with memorials or ownership. From the end of the 11c, runes began to be replaced by the Roman alphabet as Christianity spread.

Invasion time-line This activity provides a visual record of the chronology of the invasions in order to avoid confusion. The children are directed to add illustrations. The completed time-line could be used at the start of the study unit as a reference point or at the end to draw strands together.

Life in Tudor times

General This unit provides an ideal opportunity for the use of portraits as an historical source. The National Portrait Gallery has postcards and posters of Tudor monarchs. English Heritage publishes *A Teacher's Guide to Using Portraits* by Susan Morris (1989), which can be adapted for use in primary schools.

Planning grid This recommends the use of drama to help children develop their understanding of monarchy, as well as a mixture of teacher presentation and individual research, using primary and secondary historical sources.

Monarchs: the two Elizabeths This links the concept of monarchy with Elizabeth I and Elizabeth II and asks the children to discuss and record similarities and differences.

The Tudor family tree This can be completed after a teacher presentation or with reference material. Cut-out pictures will ensure that children who have difficulty with higher-order reading skills will be able to complete the task.

The *Golden Hind* In this activity, the children are asked to label the different decks on an Elizabethan ship, as well as finding out about the hierarchy on board. They can also use reference material to find out more about Sir Francis Drake and his voyages.

Inventories When someone died, an inventory was taken of their property. The example here is of a farmer who lived just outside Liverpool. The exercise shows the children what few possessions most people had in Tudor times. Several National Trust properties hold inventories from Tudor times, which would give the children an opportunity to find out how the rich people lived.

Women in Tudor times This activity encourages the children to compare gender roles now and in the past. Use it to stimulate a discussion of the difficulties professional women have traditionally encountered.

Breakfast with Queen Elizabeth I This is an example of what rich Elizabethans ate for breakfast. Compare the menu with what the children themselves ate that morning and discuss what the poorer Elizabethan people might have eaten.

A Tudor kitchen This links with the previous activity to provide information about the preparation of food in a wealthy household.

Religion in Tudor times This sheet explores the changes in religion during Tudor times and encourages the children to look in reference books to record what these changes were over 100 years of Tudor rule.

Elizabeth's advice to Mary Queen of Scots This extract comes from a letter sent by Elizabeth to Mary Queen of Scots when Mary's second husband, Henry, was found strangled in Edinburgh. Mary was later imprisoned and accused of involvement in the murder.

A Tudor house The illustration was taken from a Tudor carved mantelpiece from Speke Hall in Liverpool. It shows William Norris, his two wives and nineteen children. The Norris family was Roman Catholic and one of the wives is holding a rosary.

Who's who? This sheet provides an opportunity for children to use reference books, encyclopaedias and CD-ROM to find out about major personalities of Tudor times.

Victorian Britain

General This study unit covers several aspects of Victorian life. Decide where to focus attention and which aspects to deal with fairly briefly. This will depend on available sources, local connections and time allocation. Other links can be made with the study unit on 'Local history'.

Planning grid The emphasis here is on what it meant to be a Victorian. Change and development would therefore be seen in the context of their effects on the people. Some issues could be explored through local records and connections, for example, problems of public health and resulting improvements.

Victorian time-line This activity encourages the children to research the chronology of important events during Victoria's reign. It gives dates and visual clues to some of the most important ones.

Victorian families The children will use their observation skills to compare a rich and a poor family. Additional pictures would be useful.

Court dwellings The children are asked to consider the effects on families of the living conditions in the slum housing that was a feature of the expanding towns.

Home sweet home This sheet provides original source material on the living conditions of the Victorian poor. The children are asked to draw the room described in the excerpts, making use of the skills of observation and interpretation.

Victorian holidays The children are required to use observation and reasoning skills to interpret evidence relating to the life of a wealthy family.

Children at work This activity provides source material on child labour. The children are asked to give their own opinions on child labour, as well as considering child labour today.

Workhouse children This original source material gives information about the diet of workhouse children. The accompanying visual source shows details of their clothing and appearance.

Victorian women The popular image of Victorian women tends to be of ladies of leisure. For many, the opposite was true as shown in the illustrations.

King Cholera The source material provides a starting point for a discussion on the lack of knowledge about the cause of the disease, its spread and the subsequent improvements in public health.

Inventions of the Victorian era The activity involves finding out who invented familiar items such as the telephone (Alexander Graham Bell); electric light bulb and gramophone (Thomas Edison); petrol-driven carriage (Karl Benz). The children are then asked to explain the effects of these inventions on people's lives.

Famous Victorians The children are asked to research famous Victorians from different walks of life: Elizabeth Fry, a pioneer of prison reform; Charles Dickens, a writer; Mrs Beeton, an author of books on cookery and household management; and Isambard Kingdom Brunel, an engineer. The children are then required to find two further examples.

Britain since 1930

General This unit provides an ideal opportunity to use original source material, starting with the children's and teachers' own experiences. It makes a good starting unit for Key Stage 2 because it provides close continuity with the Programme of Study at Key Stage 1; or an ideal unit at the end of Key Stage 2 as it is possible to ensure a wide range of primary source material. This enables recording and assessment to take place as part of practical activities and provides evidence of skills acquisition since Year 3.

Planning grid Two different approaches have been suggested here. Approach A takes each decade and uses source material to explore the various themes. Approach B takes particular themes, such as transport, leisure or school, and follows them through from 1930 to the present day. Both approaches can be taught moving forwards or backwards chronologically. World War II is treated as a separate theme.

Key events time-line This time-line should be used at the start of the unit and then again at the end. It provides a means of recording the children's knowledge of the period before and after having studied it. The section that asks the children how they decided which events to include raises several questions about what makes history and whose history is recorded.

The Holocaust One of the major challenges of tackling some past events is their sheer horror. If we give the children a completely sanitised version of the past we fail to provide them with the tools of experience. In some communities the Holocaust will have much greater significance than in others, but we know that past horrors have a lesson for the present and future.

Nazi education The illustration shows how the German education system supported the Nazi propaganda, linking love and obedience to parents with love and obedience to the Führer. Some children will be able to link this activity with the previous one to show how the educational system prepared the route to the Holocaust.

The Blitz This sheet provides an opportunity to research one of the effects of the World War II on everyday life. Oral histories are particularly useful here as they provide the human stories behind the photographs of bombed buildings.

Evacuation This is taken from one person's memory of being evacuated. There are many other accounts of the experiences of evacuees.

Wartime persuasion: evacuation The children are asked to look at the techniques used to persuade people to evacuate their children to the country and to look at other wartime posters.

Staying at home This extract from Michael Foreman's *War Boy* provides a particularly vivid picture of how his widowed mother stored goods for her shop.

Identity cards for the under-sixteens The children might like to discuss the whole issue of identity cards and the reasons for them. This could be linked to the documents needed for identification today such as credit cards, driving licences, passports, etc.

Rationing This is a fairly familiar way of looking at daily life during and after the war. Food and clothing shortages are still common in many parts of the world and older children could discuss ways in which limited supplies are distributed today.

The armed forces This sheet looks at women in the armed forces. The telegram shows evidence of the call-up in 1939 and the 'Notice to Join' provides an opportunity to search for clues from a written source.

At sea This part of a transcript from a former seaman's memories of the war years shows the children how those who fought in the war felt and how, many years later, they can recall these feelings vividly.

Ancient Greece

General This unit is dependent on secondary historical sources, many of which are difficult for primary pupils to understand. The use of pictures of ruined temples, cracked pottery and misshapen coins can leave them with little feeling for the glory that was Ancient Greece. Children who live near towns where there are civic buildings modelled on Greek ones could be encouraged to see the architectural link.

Planning grid This suggests using Greek myths to introduce the topic. Pupils may be already familiar with some of these from Key Stage 1 and their own reading. The story of Troy and the wanderings of Odysseus provide a good context for the study of Ancient Greece.

Greece today This sheet provides a geographical context for historical work. You could use a map of air routes from the UK to Greece to show how we can travel today to Greece. If pupils have experiences of visiting Greece they can share these with the class.

The Greek world of myths and legends This provides a contrast to the 'real map' of the previous sheet. The places shown exist, but are linked with famous myths and legends.

Mapping the Ancient Greek world The map moves on from the world of myths and legends into the reality of the Ancient Greek civilization. It shows the extent of Greek expansion and provides an opportunity to locate places associated with important aspects of life in Ancient Greece.

A time-ribbon of key events The illustration shows a time-line running from 1000BC to AD1. Young children will need help to understand the terms Anno Domini and 'before Christ' and the way in which the BC dates become 'smaller' as they approach AD. Older children could use reference books to add other events to the time-ribbon. A much larger version of this activity could be used for display purposes.

Famous Greeks This activity provides an opportunity to use reference books to find out about famous Greeks.

The 1992 Olympic Games This activity compares the Olympic Games today with those in the past. The children should use reference books to find out more about the games and should note that in Ancient Greece separate games were held for men and women.

Vase paintings these are an important source of evidence about everyday life in Ancient Greece. There are plenty of other examples which the children can find in reference books or on a visit to a museum.

Evidence from Ancient Greece This sheet shows how to categorise the different types of evidence about ancient history. A similar exercise could be used if Ancient Egypt is chosen for the study unit 'A past non-European society'.

Ships and shipping Contrast the differences between merchant ships and warships.

The Greek alphabet This activity introduces the idea that classical languages, such as Greek, have influenced the English language. It provides an opportunity to make acquaintance with the roots of English and the fun of playing with words.

Technology problem from Ancient Greece This sheet should be used with photographs of the artefacts. The challenge to solve the problem then becomes more immediate.

A past non-European society – The Aztecs

General Sources for this study unit require careful selection to ensure full coverage of life in pre-Colombian America, as well as the European perspective of conquest and colonisation. Most of the activity sheets relate directly to the Aztecs and, where possible, original source material has been used. Other starting points could include a topical example of exploration or a collection of products that originated in the New World (eg chocolate, turkeys, tomatoes, peppers, maize, avocados, pineapples, potatoes, tobacco, spices). Links can be made with the study unit 'Life in Tudor times'.

Planning grid The focus of this approach is on the Aztec civilisation which should be investigated before looking at the explorations to stress the presence of existing cultures before the arrival of Columbus and Cortés.

The world in 1450 This activity helps the children appreciate the lack of accurate knowledge about the world in the mid-15c. The map is based on Ptolemy's *Guide to Geography* which was first published in AD150 and revived in 15c.

Exploration time-line During this period knowledge of the world was greatly extended through expeditions. The examples included are: Columbus 1492 – New World; Cabot 1497 – Newfoundland; da Gama 1497/8 – India; Magellan 1519/22 – trans-world.

Columbus and his crew This sheet involves research into historical vocabulary and the composition of the ship's crew. The examples included are: boatswain (ensured men carried out orders); caulker (carried out repairs to the ship's timbers); Royal Controller of Accounts (kept track of expenses and ensured the Crown's share of gold and land); marshal (responsible for punishing crew members); interpreter (spoke Hebrew and Arabic); secretary (wrote down official proceedings); surgeon (medical officer and naturalist) and the ship's boy.

The Old World meets the New The illustrations provide two different accounts of the same event (Columbus reaching land), inviting comparison of historical sources.

Aztec life The range of historical sources on the Aztecs is limited. Pictorial records, such as that on which the illustration on this page is based, give valuable clues to Aztec life (appearance, clothes, everyday objects). On the left, merchants sell their goods at an open market; on the right, a priest is showing glyph writing to a group of boys.

Aztec men at work As with the previous activity, the children are asked to observe aspects of everyday life. The illustration shows a goldsmith, warriors and farmers, all male. Women's life centred on the home and marriages were arranged.

Clues from the ground The children have to identify the following three objects: pottery flute; domestic pottery dish; stone knife with mosaic handle representing an Eagle Knight, used to cut out the heart of human sacrifices.

Aztec writing This sheet asks the children to design their own glyphs similar to the examples of Aztec ones and to consider the advantages and disadvantages of this system of communication. The Aztecs used picture writing in their almanacs, tribute rolls and 'histories'. Priests instructed youths in the system of glyphs.

Problems: it was difficult to use pictures to make general statements or express abstract ideas; exact, careful drawing was essential to ensure correct meaning; picture writing takes up a lot of time and room.

Advantages: the surviving examples give details about the Aztecs' life and way of representing the world.

Aztec gods The children use source material to design their own representations of Aztec gods. The Aztecs worshipped many different gods and believed in good and evil forces of nature. Worship involved offerings, including human sacrifice, prayers and the performance of symbolic acts in the presence of priests.

The defeat of the Aztecs This sheet requires the children to identify some of the reasons for the rapid defeat of the Aztecs.

Clues in the pictures: Spanish weapons superior (eg guns, cannons, crossbows); steel armour gave protection against Aztec weapons (eg wooden clubs, javelins, bows and arrows); the Spanish brought horses to form cavalry while the Aztecs fought on foot.

Additional reasons: Aztec warriors were not drilled in the way that Spanish soldiers were, Aztec warfare was traditionally highly ceremonial; Cortés arrived at harvest time when attention was focused on crops rather than fighting; revolts and intrigue were rife within the Aztec Empire; Montezuma was slow to respond, influenced by Aztec prophecies; susceptibility to diseases brought by the Spaniards from the Old World.

The effects of exploration The children should consider the impact of the explorations on the New World (the Aztec Empire) and the Old (Spain), and give their own views.

Impact on the Aztec Empire: end of the Aztec civilisation; forced conversion to Christianity; loss of land; slave labour in mines and on haciendas; new diseases killing thousands; introduction of new technology (eg wheel, iron); domesticated animals introduced (eg horses, cows, sheep).

Impact on Spain: empire extended; gold and wealth to boost royal coffers; Spanish power and status increased; new products introduced (eg potatoes, tomatoes, turkeys, peppers, maize, tobacco); increased trade.

Support materials

General These sheets have been designed specifically for use with the Key Stage 2 materials, but several of them could be adapted for use at Key Stage 1.

Teacher planning grid This is an adapted version of that provided by the NCC in the original non-statutory guidance. It was found that this was of more direct use for overall planning as it linked directly with pupil assessment and record keeping.

Pupil record sheet The headings are expanded to enable parents to understand exactly what their children have undertaken. As the teacher's original plan is duplicated for each pupil, it enables absences and the level of work undertaken to be noted.

Resource evaluation: teacher's sheets (1) and (2) These sheets could be used on a school or year basis to provide information on each study unit.

Pupil ideas sheet and **Pupil comment sheet** These are intended to involve the children directly in the overall planning and evaluation of study units. On the first one the children's questions may involve adaptation of the original planning grid.

History detectives: using the evidence, **Investigating an artefact** and **Our class museum** These sheets examine directly the skills required to classify and interpret historical sources.

Time-line and **Time-ribbon** These sheets provide two different ways of developing the children's sense of chronology. Both time-lines have been left blank so that pupils of all ages can use them.

Interview schedule Provides support material for children interviewing adults about the past.

(See inside back cover for Scottish 5-14 Curriculum and Northern Ireland Curriculum links)

Name _____

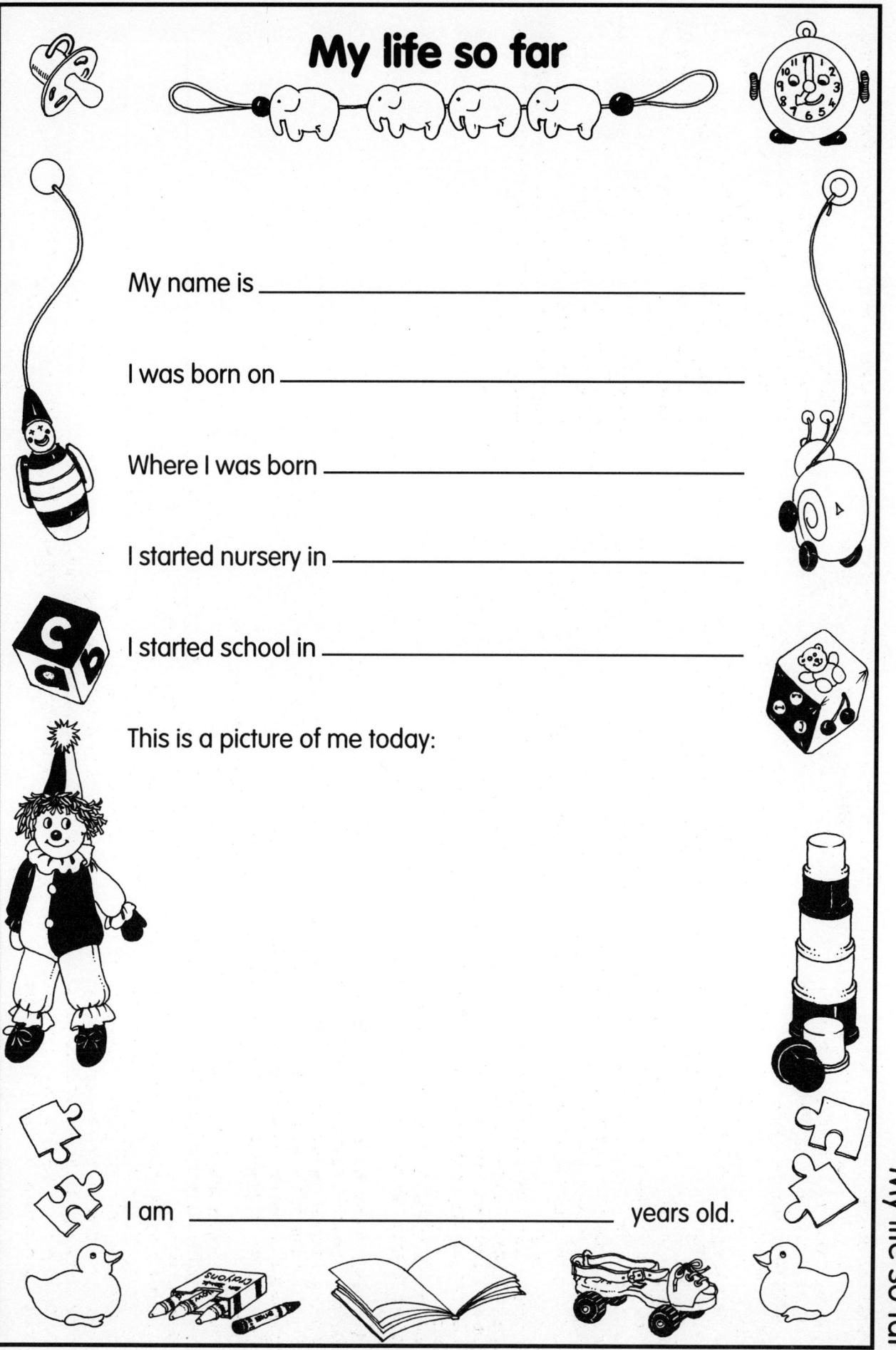

All about me

My life so far

My life so far

My name is _____

I was born on _____

Where I was born _____

I started nursery in _____

I started school in _____

This is a picture of me today:

I am _____ years old.

History 13

All about me

My family

Name _____

My family

✤ Draw your family.

✤ Who is in the picture? _____

_____

_____

History

Name _____

All about me

My favourite things

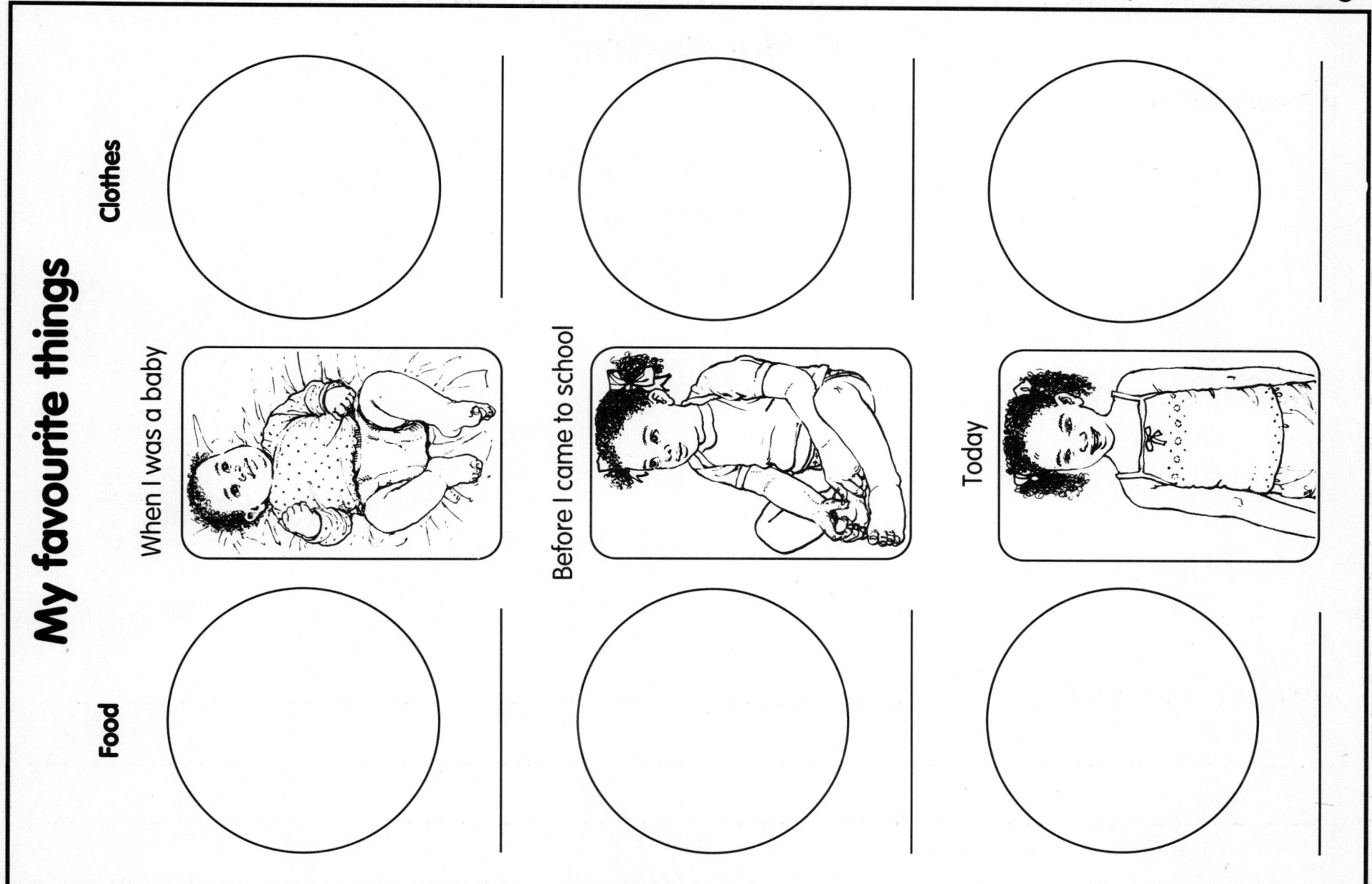

History 15

All about me
A family tree

Name _____

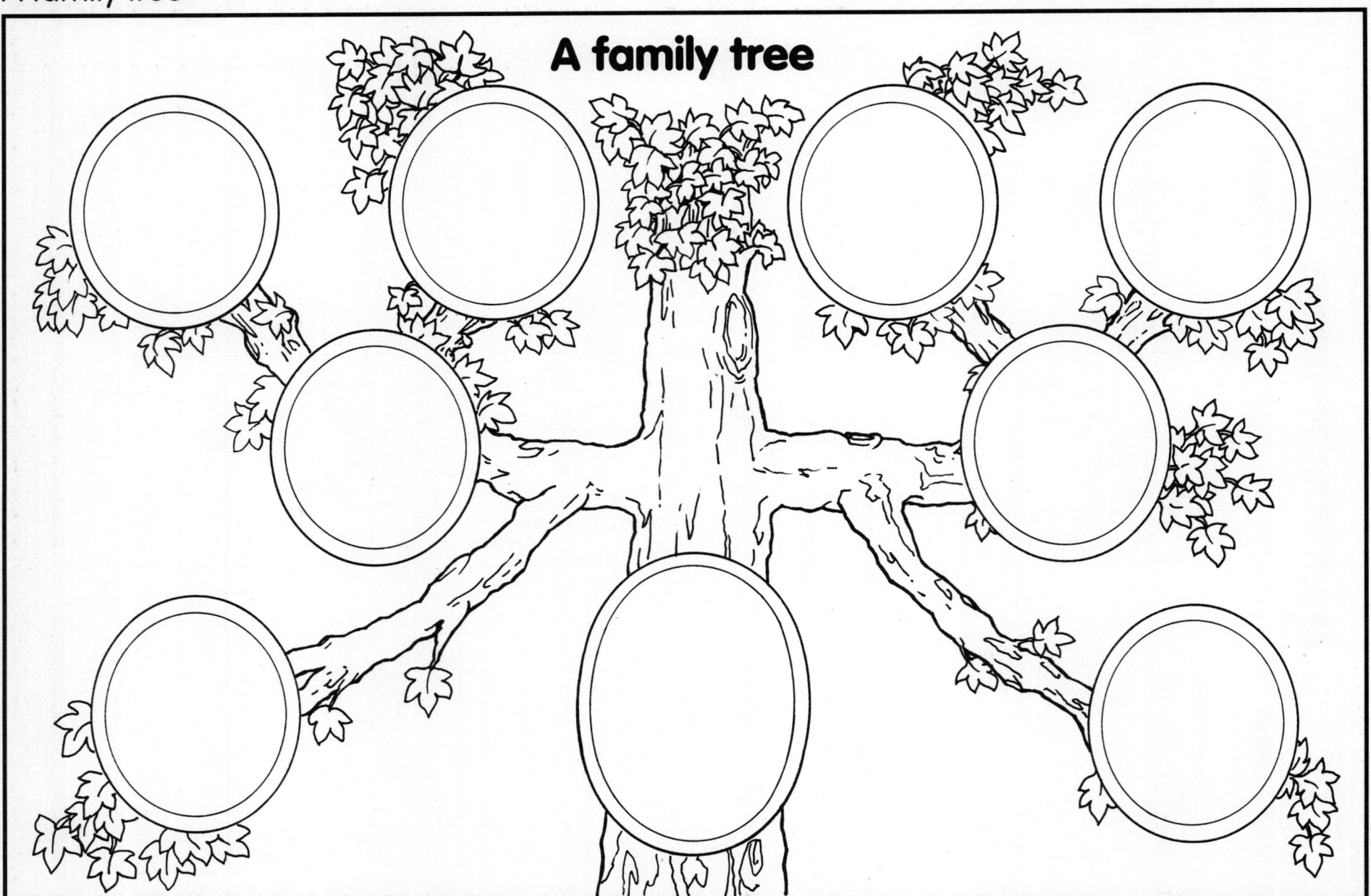

Name _____

All about me

A generation circle

A generation circle

- Older people and grandparents
- Grown-ups in my family
- Children in my family

Older people

Grown-ups

Children

History

All about me

The generation game

Name _____

♣ Match the objects to the members of the family who would use them.

18
History

Name _____

All about me

My patchwork quilt of memories

My patchwork quilt of memories

✤ Draw or write what you remember happened at the time.

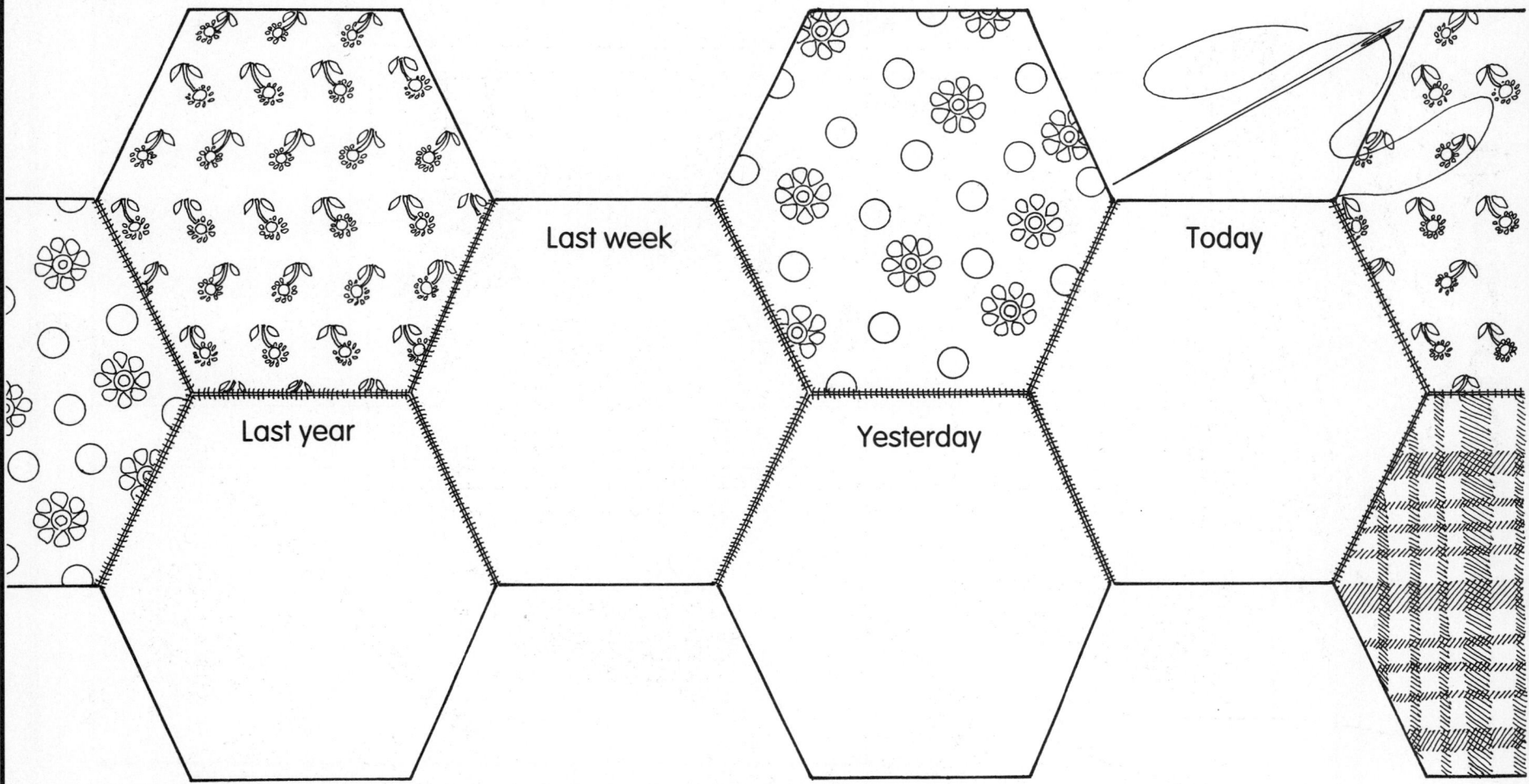

- Last week
- Today
- Last year
- Yesterday

✤ Do you know what a patchwork quilt is? Can you find out?

History

19

All about me
Childhood memories

Name _____

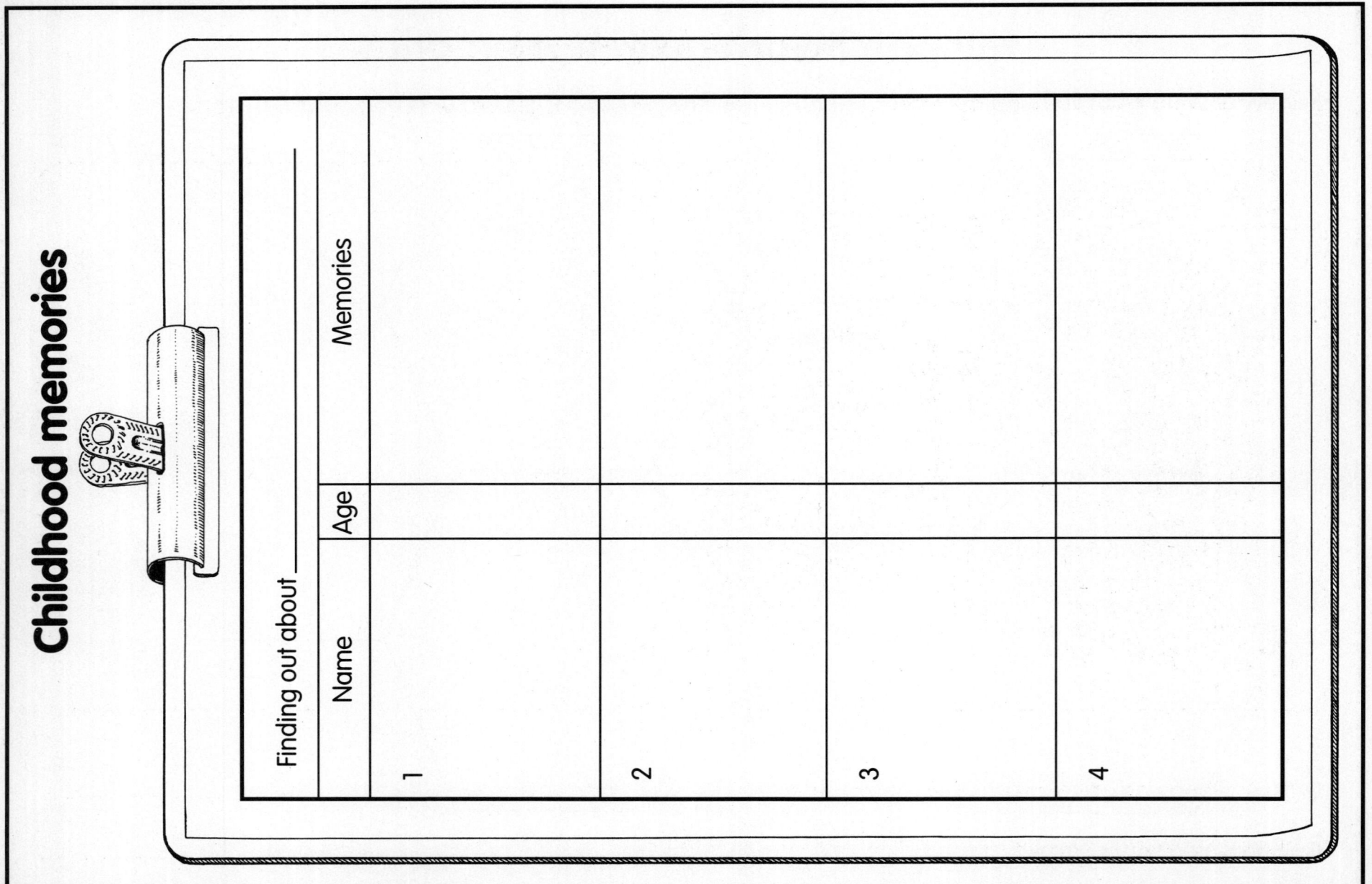

Childhood memories

Finding out about _____

Name	Age	Memories
1		
2		
3		
4		

Name _____

People

People in school

People in school

Below is a picture of a 1900s classroom.

✤ Draw a picture of your classroom today.

✤ These things are the same _____

✤ These things are different _____

History

21

People

People in fairy-tales

Name _____

People in fairy-tales

♣ Who slept for 100 years?   ♣ Who wore a glass slipper?   ♣ Whose cat made him a fortune?

Name _____

People

People in legends

People in legends

♣ Which king had a sword called Excalibur?

_____

♣ Who lived in Sherwood Forest?

_____

♣ Which Biblical queen saved the Jews from the Persians?

_____

History

People
The Royal Family

Name _____

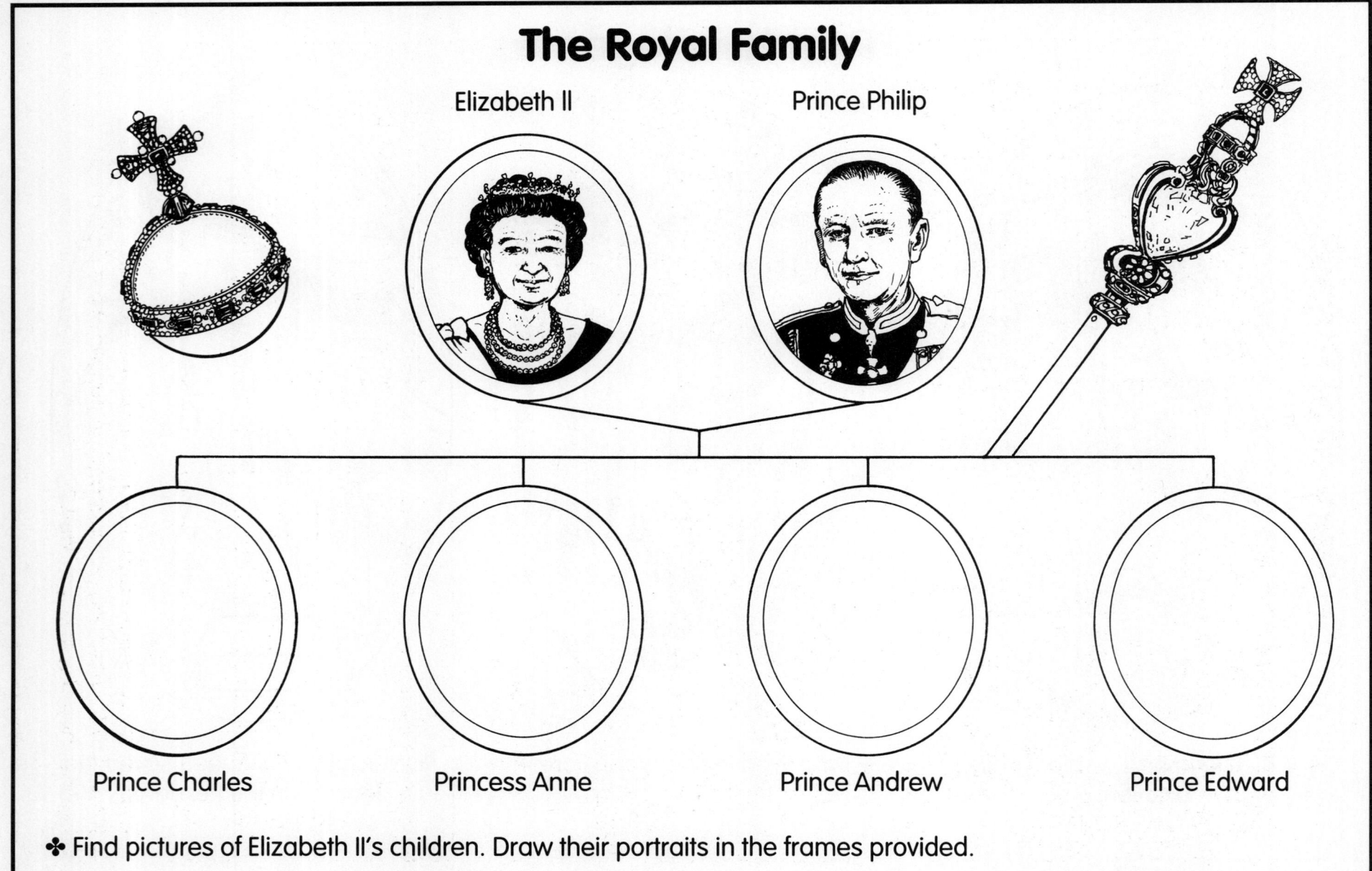

The Royal Family

Elizabeth II Prince Philip

Prince Charles Princess Anne Prince Andrew Prince Edward

❖ Find pictures of Elizabeth II's children. Draw their portraits in the frames provided.

History

Name _____

People

The story of St Patrick

He returned to Ireland and converted many people to Christianity.

Later he escaped and became a priest.

After he died he was made a saint.

When Patrick was a boy he was captured by Irish pirates.

✤ Cut out the sentences and match them to the pictures.
✤ Now put the matching pictures and sentences in the right order.
✤ Do you think this is a true story?

History

25

People

Name _____

Harriet Tubman: a legend in her time

She escaped from slavery and made the long journey north.

She returned to the South and rescued many slaves.

Harriet Tubman was born a slave in America.

She grew up to hate slavery and began to fight against it.

✤ Cut out the sentences and match them to the pictures.
✤ Now put the matching sentences and pictures in the right order.
✤ Do you think this is a true story?

26

History

Name _____

People

Famous nurses

Famous nurses

This is a picture of Mary Seacole, a famous nurse who helped soldiers in the Crimean War.

♣ Use reference books to find out about another nurse and write about her here.

History

27

People

Famous children

Name _____

Famous children

Anne Frank   **Wolfgang Amadeus Mozart**

  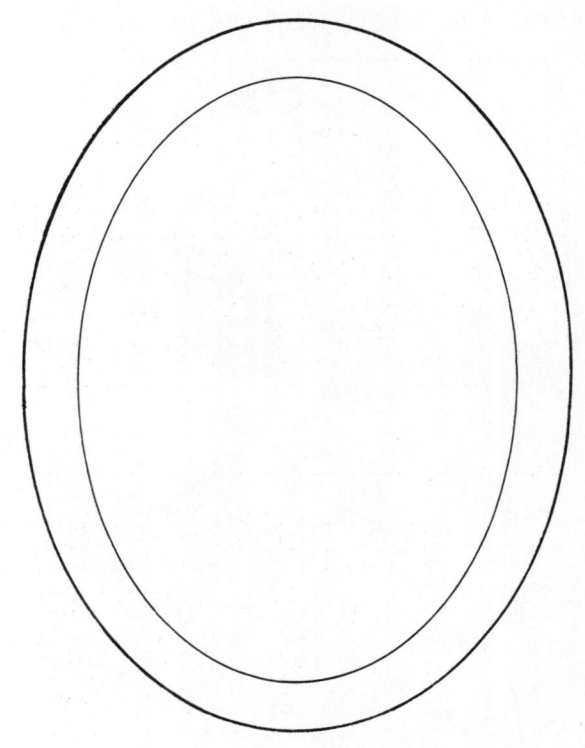

♣ Anne Frank was famous because _____

♣ Mozart was famous because _____

♣ Can you think of another famous child? Draw his or her picture in the empty frame and explain why he or she was famous.

28   History

Name _____

Places
Name the buildings

Name the buildings

This is a _____

This is a _____

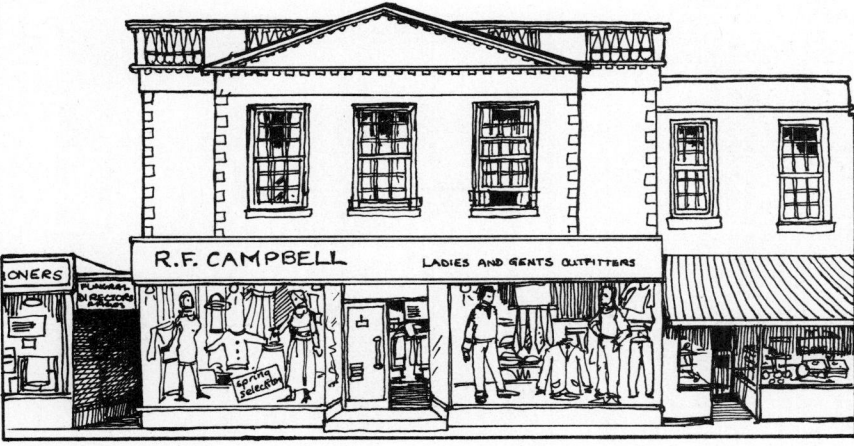

This is a _____

This is a _____

Places

What has changed?

What has changed?

The three pictures below show the same house at different times.
♣ Put a ring round the things that have changed.

1930

1960

Today

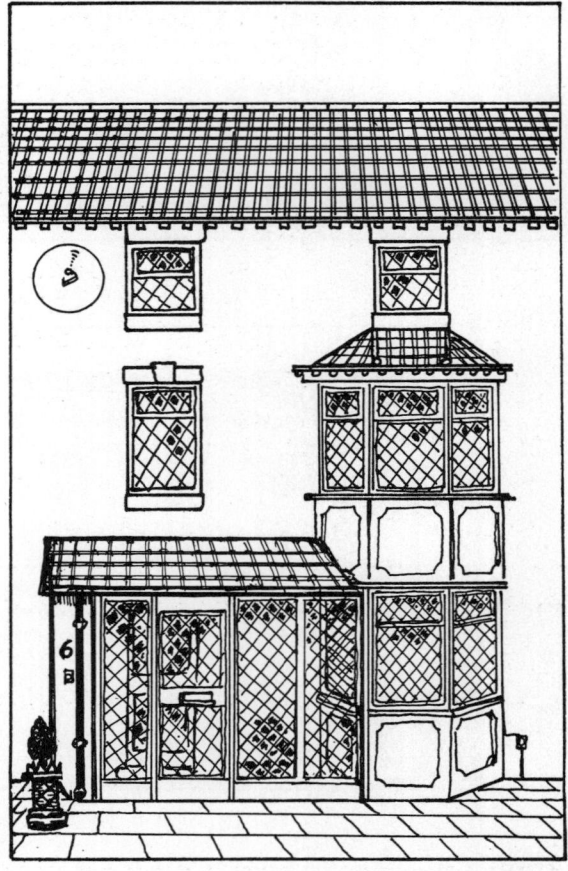

Name _____

Places

In the bedroom: then and now

In the bedroom: then and now

This is a child's bedroom in the past.

♣ Draw a child's bedroom today.

♣ Find three things that are different. Write about them here.

1 _____

2 _____

3 _____

Places

In the street: then and now

In the street: then and now

In the past   **Today**

✤ In which picture do these objects belong?

    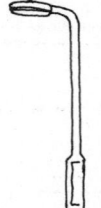 

History

Name _____

Places

At the shops: then and now

At the shops: then and now

In the past

Today

♣ Look at the pictures. Find three things that are different. Write about them here.

1 _____
2 _____
3 _____

History

Places

A homes time-line (1)

Name _____

A homes time-line (1)

♣ Cut out the pictures and make a homes time-line.

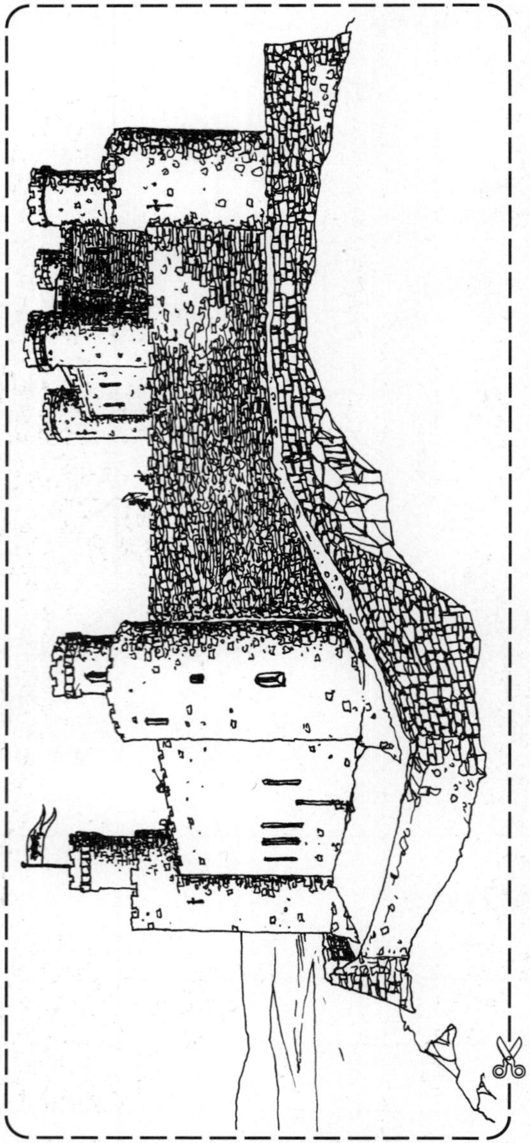

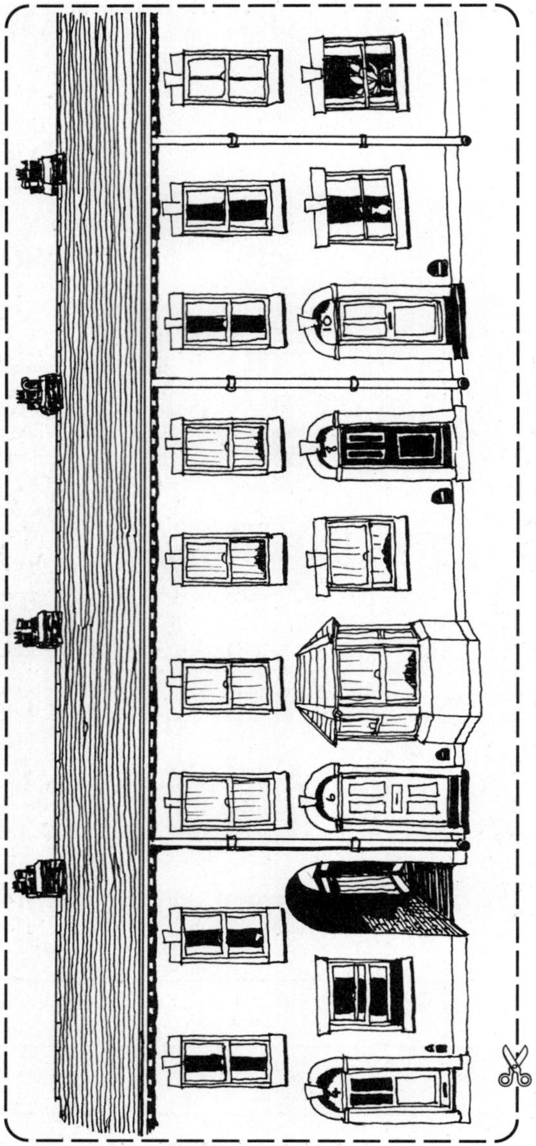

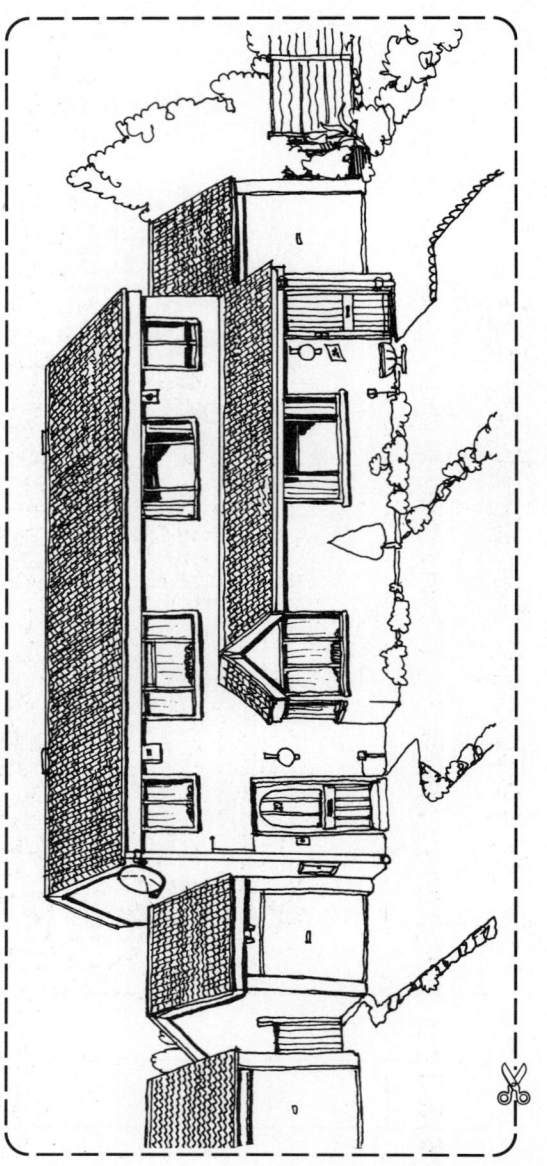

34

History

Name _____

Places

A homes time-line (2)

A homes time-line (2)

♣ Cut out the pictures and make a homes time-line.

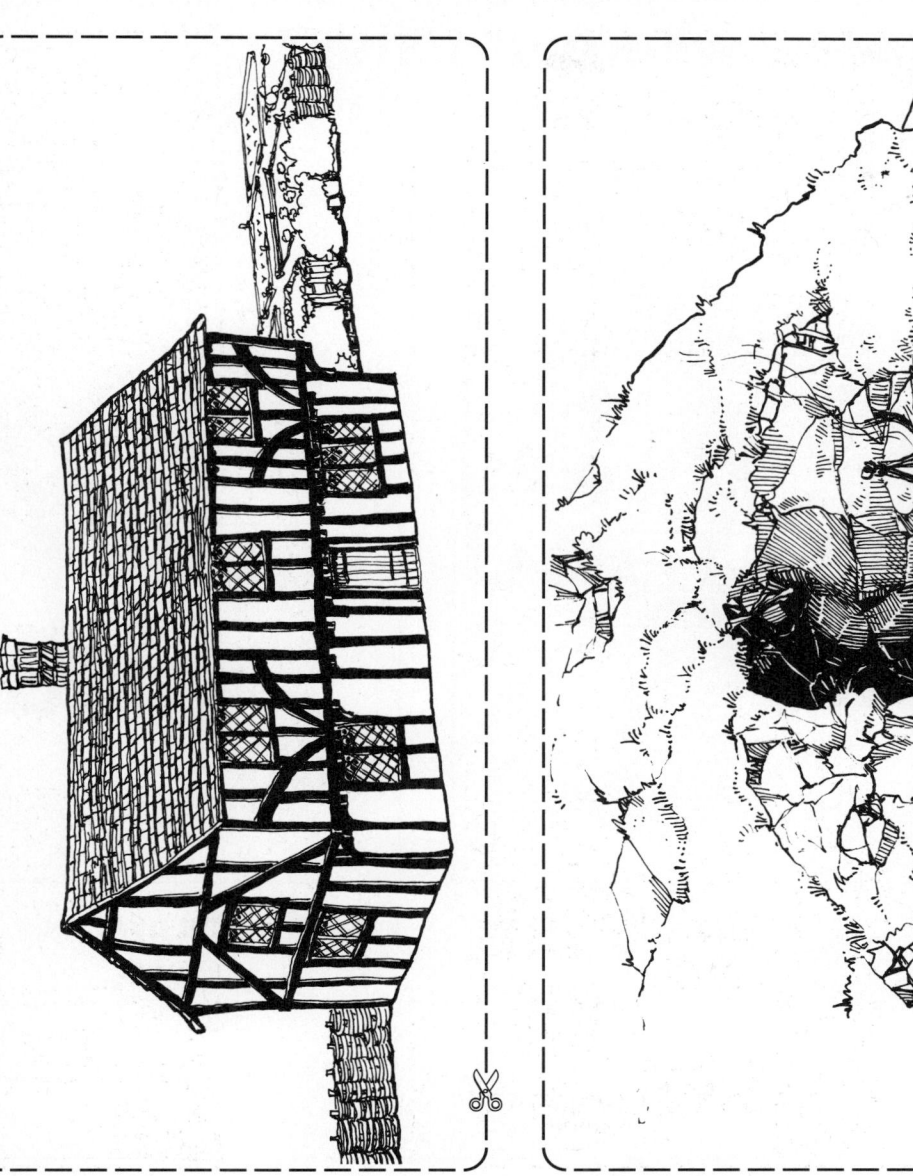

History

35

Places

Famous places: where are they?

Name _____

Famous places: where are they?

Disneyland

Taj Mahal

The pyramids

♣ This is in _____

♣ This is in _____

♣ This is in _____

♣ Which is the oldest? _____

36

History

Name _____

Celebrations

What does your family celebrate?

What does your family celebrate?

♣ What does your family celebrate?

Celebration	This is how we celebrate

Passover Diwali Ramadan

Chinese New Year Christmas

History

Celebrations

Name _____

Christmas

♣ Christmas is one of the most important Christian festivals. It celebrates the birth of _____

♣ What sorts of things does Christmas make you think of? Draw and write about them in the box below.

38

History

Name _____

Celebrations

Birthday celebrations

Birthday celebrations

This is a picture of a birthday party 100 years ago.

♣ Draw a picture of your own last birthday party in the frame below.

History

39

Celebrations

Birthday greetings

Name _____

Birthday greetings

This is how birthday cards looked 100 years ago.

♣ Draw a birthday card that you could buy today.

Birthday Greetings

♣ I can see

_____
_____
_____

♣ I have drawn

_____
_____
_____

History

Name _____

Celebrations

Special occasions

Special occasions

This mug was made for a special event.

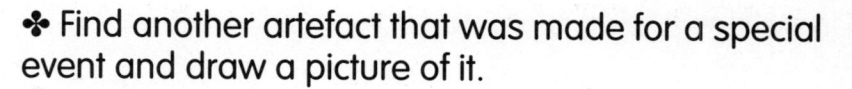

✤ Find another artefact that was made for a special event and draw a picture of it.

✤ What was the event? _____
✤ What was the date? _____

✤ What was the event? _____
✤ What was the date? _____

History

41

Celebrations

Matching artefacts

Name _____

Matching artefacts

✤ Draw lines joining each object to its name.

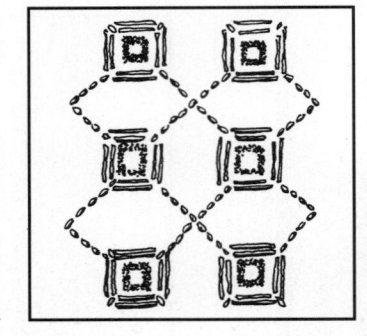

| Fireworks | Sweetmeats | Lakshmi Puja | Rangoli patterns | Diwali lights |

✤ Find out what happens during Diwali and write about it here.

_____
_____
_____

History

Name _____

Celebrations

A spring myth

A spring myth

♣ Look at the pictures below. They tell a story. Finish the story by drawing a picture and writing a sentence.

1 Persephone was gathering flowers in the meadow.

2 The god of the underworld carried her away.

3 She was queen of the underworld for six months of the year.

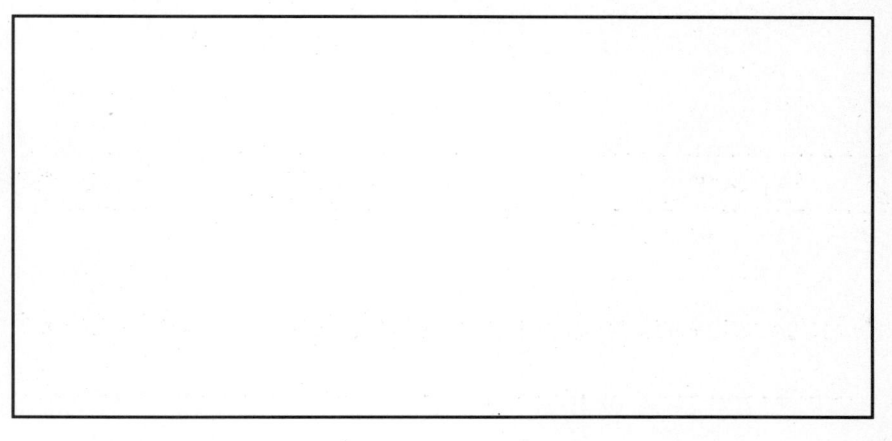

4 _____

History

Celebrations

Easter eggs

Name _____

Easter eggs

✤ In many countries, people celebrate Easter with brightly painted eggs. Decorate your own Easter eggs.

44

History

Name _____

Fun and games

My favourite toys

My favourite toys

When I was a baby	When I could walk	Before I came to school	Now

History

45

Fun and games

Name _____

Toys: then and now

Toys: then and now

♣ Decide which is your favourite toy and draw it in the space below.

♣ Now ask an older person about his or her favourite toy. Draw it in the space below.

♣ Write the names of your other favourite toys.

_____
_____
_____

I asked _____

His or her other favourite toys were _____
_____
_____
_____

History

Name _____

Fun and games

Children's books: then and now

Children's books: then and now

The picture below is from a 1930s children's book.
♣ What can you see in the picture?

♣ Draw a picture from your favourite book in the space provided. Is it like the 1930s book?

History

47

Fun and games

Name _____

Playing outside: then and now

Playing outside: then and now

✤ Look at these Victorian children playing outside. What are they playing with?

✤ In the box below draw children playing outside today.

Name _____

Fun and games

Playground rhymes

Playground rhymes

In the past

Ring o' roses

Ring a ring o' roses,
A pocket full of posies
A-tishoo, a-tishoo,
We all fall down.

Ashes in the water,
Ashes in the sea,
We all jump up
With a one, two, three.

Today

❖ What is your favourite playground rhyme? Write it on the page above.
❖ What other rhymes do you know?

History

49

Fun and games

A toyshop in the past

Name _____

A toyshop in the past

♣ Look at the picture. Say what is wrong. Put a ring round the toys that would not have been there.

50

History

Name _____

Fun and games

Make a doll time-line

Make a doll time-line

♣ Make a doll time-line. Ask some older people what their dolls were like.

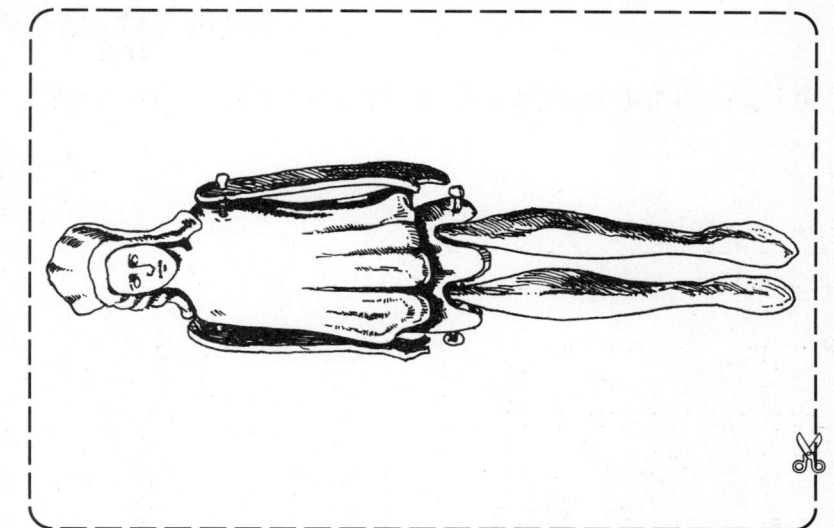

History

51

Fun and games

Name _____

Make a games time-line

Make a games time-line

✤ Cut out the pictures and make a games time-line. Can you add other games played in the past to your time-line?

52

History

Name _____

Travel

Going places

Going places

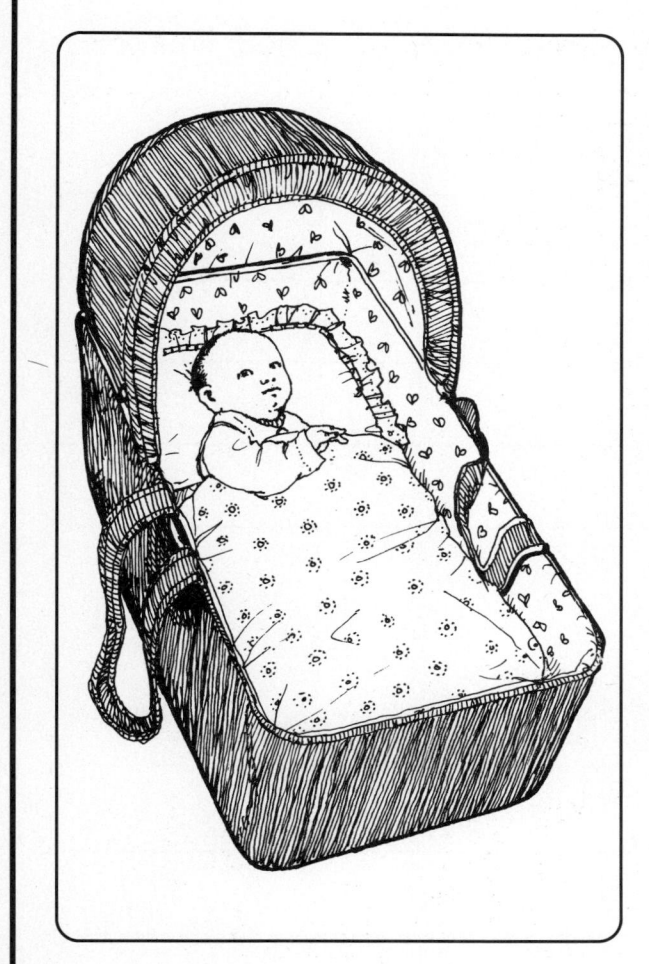

Babies travel in
_____

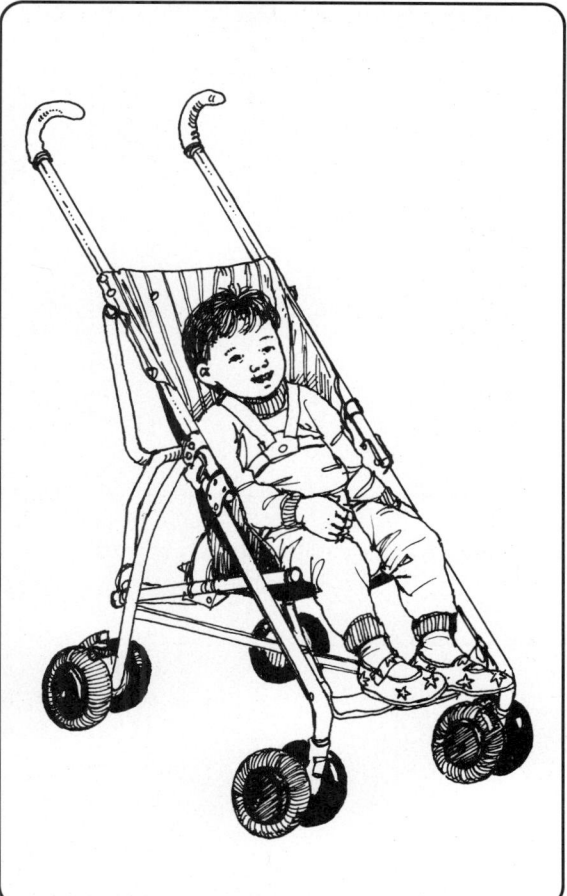

Toddlers travel in
_____

I travel in
_____

History

53

Travel

Name _____

Going to school: then and now

Going to school: then and now

✤ How do you travel to school? Draw and write about it here.

✤ Now ask someone a lot older than you how he or she used to travel to school. Draw and write about it here.

54 History

Name _____

Travel

A pram time-line

A pram time-line

✤ Cut out the pictures and make a time-line.

✤ See if you can find photographs showing old prams.
Who will you ask to help you?

History

Travel

Name _____

In the Transport Museum

In the Transport Museum

♣ What can you see in the Transport Museum?

_____

_____

_____

♣ See if you can find photographs or illustrations of these vehicles.

History

Name _____

Travel

Famous travellers

Famous travellers

♣ Match the traveller with the country they explored. Find the countries on a globe.

Mary Kingsley **Marco Polo** **Christopher Columbus**

The Americas **Africa** **China**

History

57

Travel

Name _____

Road transport time-line

Road transport time-line

❖ Colour the pictures. Cut them out and make a time-line.

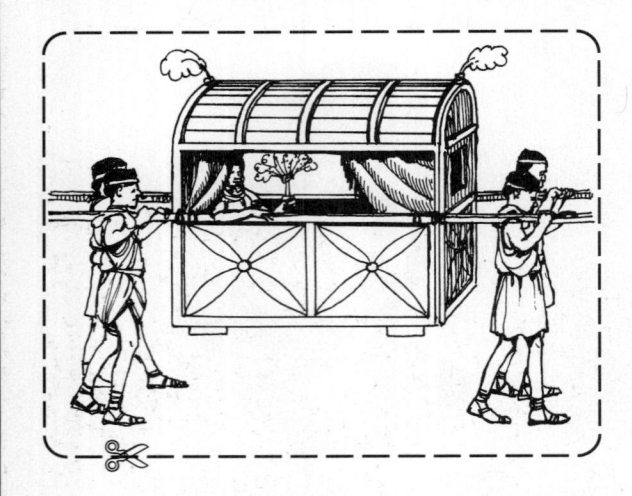

❖ Make a collection of pictures and photographs of these types of transport.

History

Name _____

Travel

Going to the seaside

Going to the seaside

Blackpool 1900

Blackpool today

✤ Write here what is the same in the two pictures.

✤ Write here what is different.

History

59

Travel

Name _____

Street furniture

Street furniture

✤ Draw a modern post-box in the empty space. Make a post-box time-line.

✤ Are there any post-boxes like these near your school?

History

Name _____

Romans, Anglo-Saxons and Vikings in Britain

Planning grid

ROMANS, ANGLO-SAXONS AND VIKINGS

KEY QUESTIONS	CONCEPTS	CONTENT	RESOURCES, TYPES OF SOURCES	ACTIVITIES, TEACHING AND LEARNING METHODS	RECORDING AND ASSESSMENT
• What was Britain like before the Romans came?	• Settlement • Tribe	• The different tribes and their location • Daily life in Pre-Roman Britain	• Maps • Reference books • Illustrations • Artefacts (museum)	• Identifying tribes on map • Group research into different aspects of Celtic life • Presentation	• Can children transfer information from sources to explain how people lived? (Oral, pictorial or written response)
Invaders: • Who were they? • When did they invade? • Why did they come? • How did they get here?	• Chronology • Invasion • Settlement • Raid • Trade • Conquest	• Invasion dates • Countries of origin • Routes taken • Reasons for invasion: trade/glory/need for land • Ship designs	• Time-lines • Maps • Travel brochures • Photographs • Reference books • Illustrations • Written accounts • Artefacts (museums)	• Sequencing key events on time-lines (individual and class) • Locating modern homelands on maps • Tracing routes to Britain • Role-playing: planning raid or settlement • Finding out historical reasons for invasions and settlements	• Can children correctly sequence invasions? • Do they show understanding of the BC/AD chronology? • Can they locate countries of origin on a map? • Can they express different points of view in role-play? • Do they use historical vocabulary correctly? • Can they extract and transfer information?
• Were there rebellions?	• Cause and consequence • Change • Conquest • Rebellion	• Celtic resistance (Boudicca) • Anglo-Saxon resistance (Alfred Hereward)	• Reference books • Written accounts • Historical fiction	• Listening to stories of resistance read by teacher • Role-playing: reaction to invasion (groups)	• Can children explain why rebellion took place? • Do they show evidence of empathy?
• What was daily life like? (choose one group of settlers only)	• Cause and consequence • Change • Similarities and differences • Settlement • Trade	• Settlements • Family life • Clothes and appearance • Occupations • Transport • Trade/money • Food and farming • Crafts • Defence • Writing • Leisure • Worship • Myths and legends	• Artefacts (museum) • Reconstructions • Photos and illustrations • Reference books • Written accounts • Historical fiction • Television programmes and video material • Recordings of recreated music	• Research: (individual or groups) using sources according to pupils abilities and displaying results • Role-playing, e.g. the saga of *Beowulf* • Holding a Roman, Anglo-Saxon or Viking day	• Can children extract and transfer information for presentation? • Do children use historical vocabulary correctly? • Can they use informed imagination to describe life in Roman, Anglo-Saxon or Viking Britain?
• What did the Romans, Anglo-Saxons and Vikings leave us?	• Continuity	• Place-names • Language • Design motifs • Julian Calendar • Ruins/sites	• Maps • Dictionary giving derivations • Items using Roman, Anglo-Saxon or Viking design, e.g. replica jewellery • Museum shop catalogues • Photographs of ceremonies, e.g. Viking festival (York)	• Working individually to find place-names with Roman, Anglo-Saxon and Viking endings • Using a dictionary to find words of Roman, Anglo-Saxon or Viking origin • Using Roman, Anglo-Saxon and Viking motifs to create artwork	• Can the children find examples of continuity between past and present?

History

61

Romans, Anglo-Saxons and Vikings in Britain

Name _____

Britain

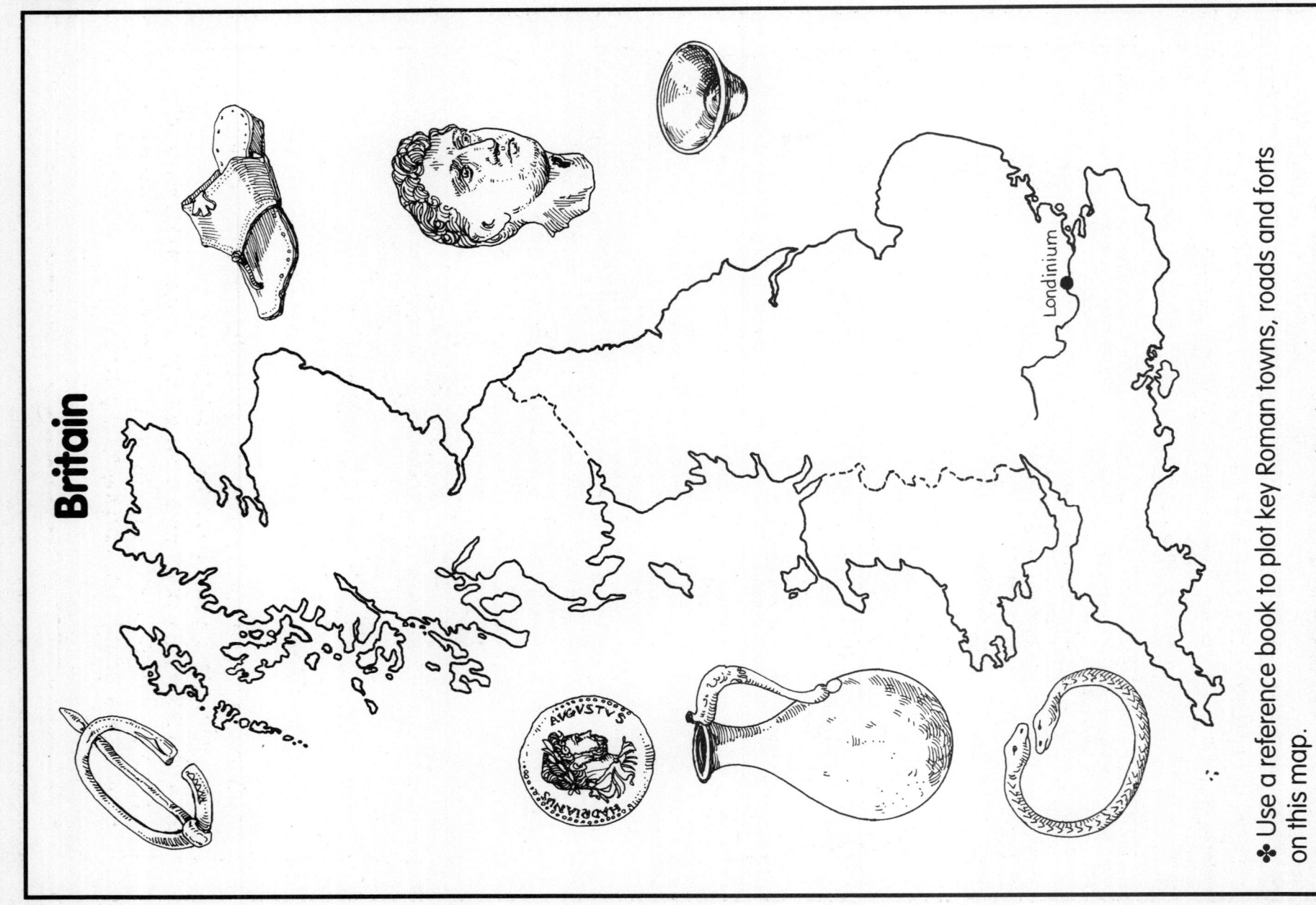

Britain

Londinium

♣ Use a reference book to plot key Roman towns, roads and forts on this map.
♣ Mark the nearest big city to your school.

AVGVSTVS HADRIANVS

62

History

Name _____

Romans, Anglo-Saxons and Vikings in Britain

Britain before the Romans

Britain before the Romans

At the time of the Roman invasion, Britain was inhabited by Celtic tribes. The map shows where the different tribes lived.

Tribes shown on map: Taezali, Vacomagi, Caledones, Epidii, Venicones, Damnonii, Selgovae, Novantae, Votadini, Brigantes, Parisi, Deceangli, Cornovii, Ordovices, Coritani, Iceni, Catuvellauni, Trinovantes, Cantii, Atrebates, Demetae, Silures, Dobunni, Durotriges, Dumnonii

♣ Mark the position of the nearest big town to your school on the map. Which tribe would you have belonged to?
♣ Find out what it would have been like if you lived in a Celtic family. On the back of this sheet, write about your family, your appearance, your clothes, your house and the food you ate.

History

63

Romans, Anglo-Saxons and Vikings in Britain

Name _____

Why bother with Britain?

Why bother with Britain?

The map below shows the countries that were part of the Roman Empire 2000 years ago. Britain had not yet been invaded.
♣ Use an atlas to find out the modern names of some of the countries that were part of the empire.

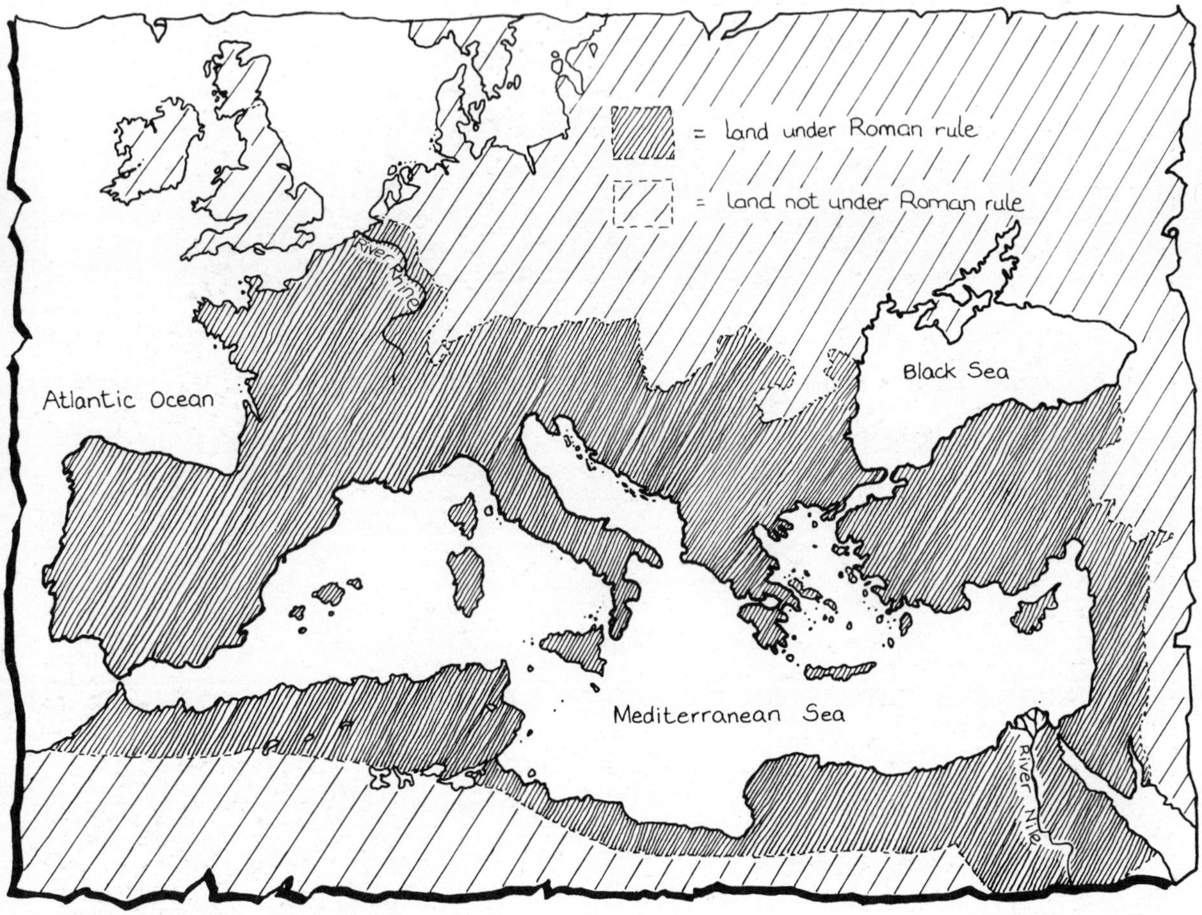

= land under Roman rule

= land not under Roman rule

After two invasions that failed, Emperor Claudius sent a larger army to Britain. The empire already covered most of Europe.
♣ Why do you think the emperor wanted to conquer Britain?

64

History

Name _____

Romans, Anglo-Saxons and Vikings in Britain

A Roman town

A Roman town

The Romans built many towns in the countries that they ruled. The picture below shows the town of Viroconium or Wroxeter. It probably began as a fort, built to defend the area against tribes from Wales.

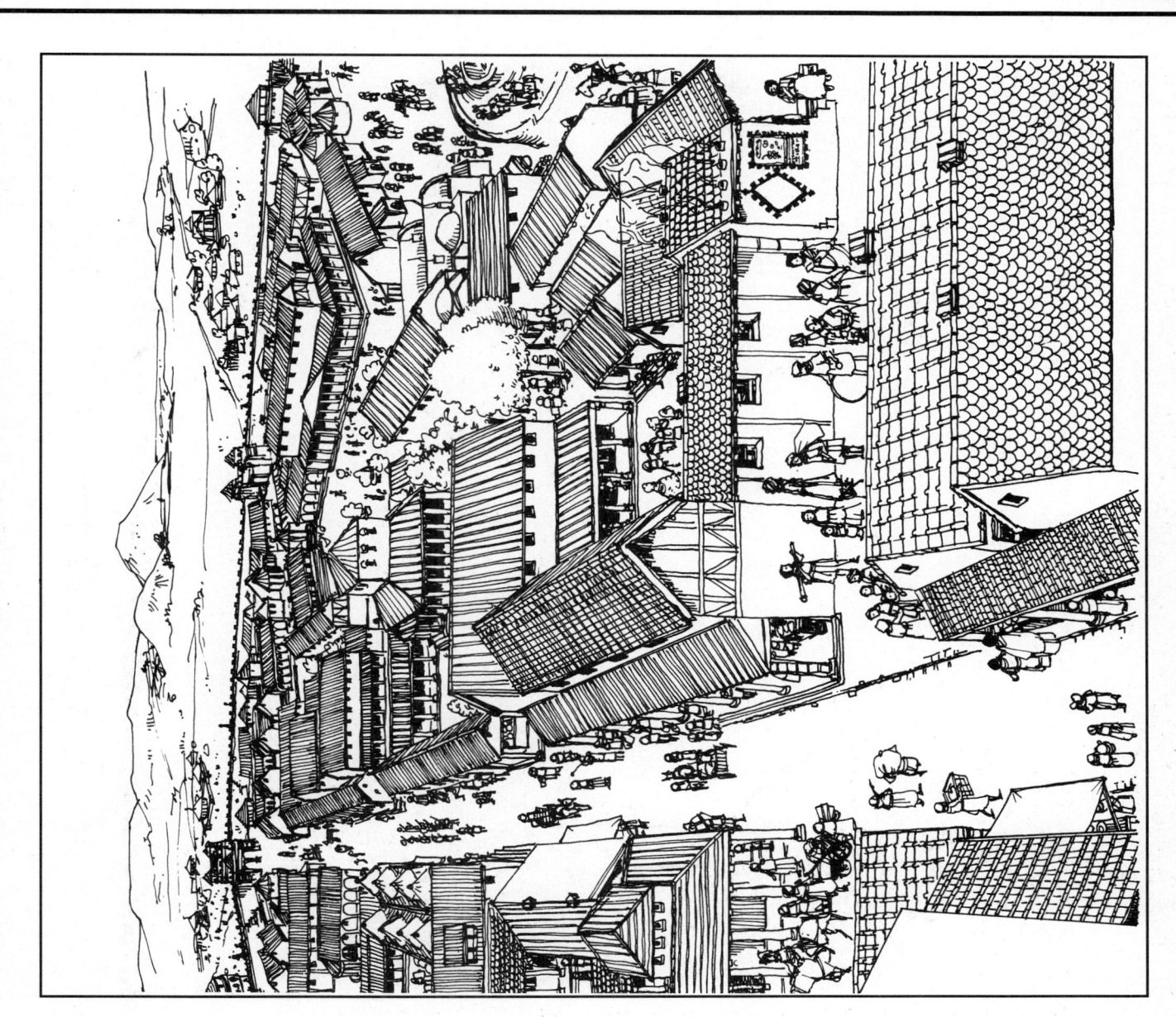

♣ What materials did the Romans use to build the town?
♣♣ What buildings would you expect to find in a Roman town?
♣ Find the names of other towns built in Britain by the Romans.

History

65

Romans, Anglo-Saxons and Vikings in Britain

Name _____

An Anglo-Saxon village

The Anglo-Saxons lived in villages. Many Roman towns became ruins as the Saxon settlers chose to build their villages where the land was good for farming. The picture below shows a 'tun' or defended village.

♣ What materials were used to build the houses?
♣ Who lived in the largest house?
♣ Why was a wall built around the settlement?

Name _____

Romans, Anglo-Saxons and Vikings in Britain

A Viking town

A Viking town

The Vikings were good farmers and keen traders. Unlike the Saxons, they were townspeople. They built new towns, such as Dublin, and took over existing ones, like York. Expert craftsmen had their workshops in the towns.

♣ What materials did the Vikings use to build the houses?
♣ What kinds of craftsmen lived in the town?
♣ Some of the streets were paved with logs. Why was this?

History

67

Romans, Anglo-Saxons and Vikings in Britain

Name _____

What's in a name?

What's in a name?

The Romans, the Saxons and the Vikings all left traces of their languages in our place-names. Place-names can help us find out where these different people once settled.
These are some of the most common place-name endings in Britain.

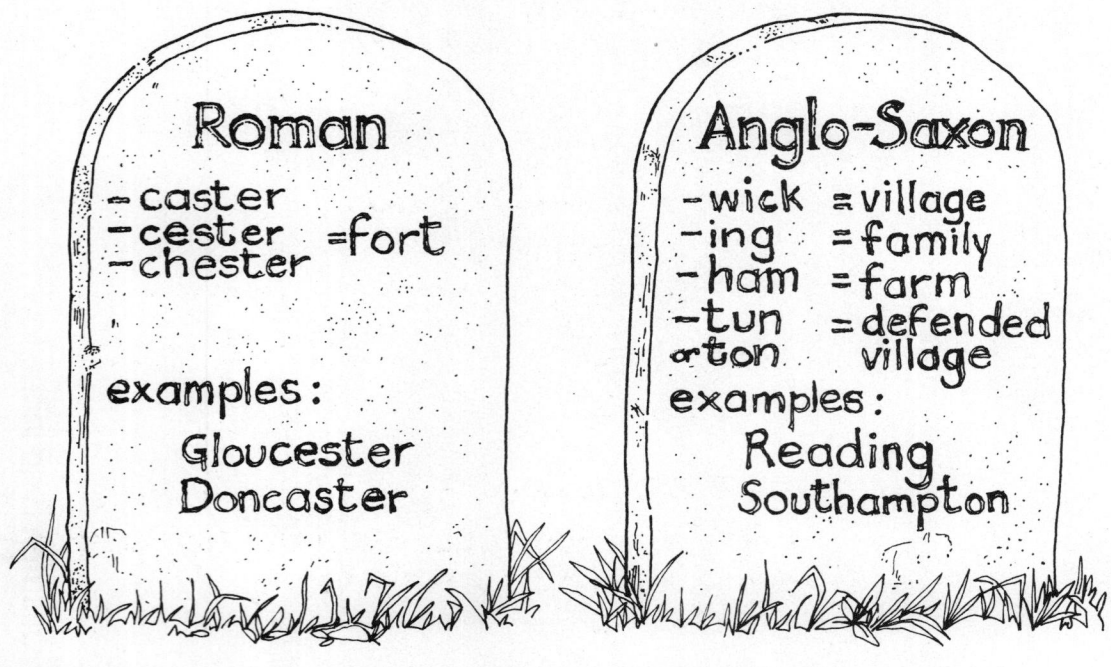

Roman
-caster
-cester = fort
-chester

examples:
Gloucester
Doncaster

Anglo-Saxon
-wick = village
-ing = family
-ham = farm
-tun
-ton = defended village

examples:
Reading
Southampton

Viking
-dale = valley
-by = farmstead
-thorpe = hamlet
-thwaite = clearing

examples:
Whitby
Borrowdale

♣ Look at a map of Britain and find examples of each type of ending.
♣ Now look at a map of your region. Which is the most common type of ending? List some examples here.

_____

♣ What does this tell you about when your area was settled?

68

History

Romans, Anglo-Saxons and Vikings in Britain

The 'three Rs' Roman style

The 'three Rs' Roman style

The Romans used the Latin alphabet for writing. We still use the same alphabet today. Here is an example of Roman writing on a tombstone.

RVFVS·SITA·EQVES·CHO VI
TRAC/M·ANN·XL·STIP·XXII
HEREDES·EXS·TEST·F CVRAVES

♣ Design a tombstone on the back of this page. Write your inscription in Roman-style letters. Remember • to • put • dots • between • the • words.

On the tombstone, you can see number 22 written in Roman style as XXII. Here are some more Roman numbers.

I – 1	IV – 4	VII – 7	X – 10
II – 2	V – 5	VIII – 8	C – 100
III – 3	VI – 6	IX – 9	

♣ Complete the sums.

IV + VI = ____   III + VII = ____

VII + I = ____   V + II = ____

♣ We still use Roman numbers today. Find some examples and record them here.

History

69

Romans, Anglo-Saxons and Vikings in Britain

Name _____

Monks and manuscripts

In Anglo-Saxon times all books had to be copied out by hand. This was done by monks writing with a metal stylus on specially treated animal skins called vellum. The monks liked to decorate some of the letters, usually the first letter on a page. Here are some examples.

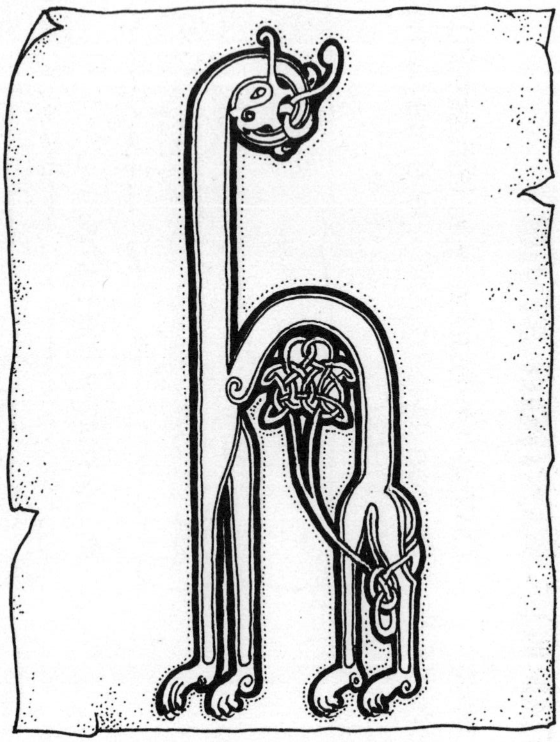

♣ Colour the letters using bright felt-tipped pens or crayons.
♣ Draw your initials below and decorate them in the same way.

Name _____

Romans, Anglo-Saxons and Vikings in Britain

Writing in runes

Writing in runes

The Vikings wrote in runes. The letters were made up of straight lines. This was because runes were carved in stone or wood. A Viking would always carry a knife, so that he could pick up a twig and carve a message in it at any time.

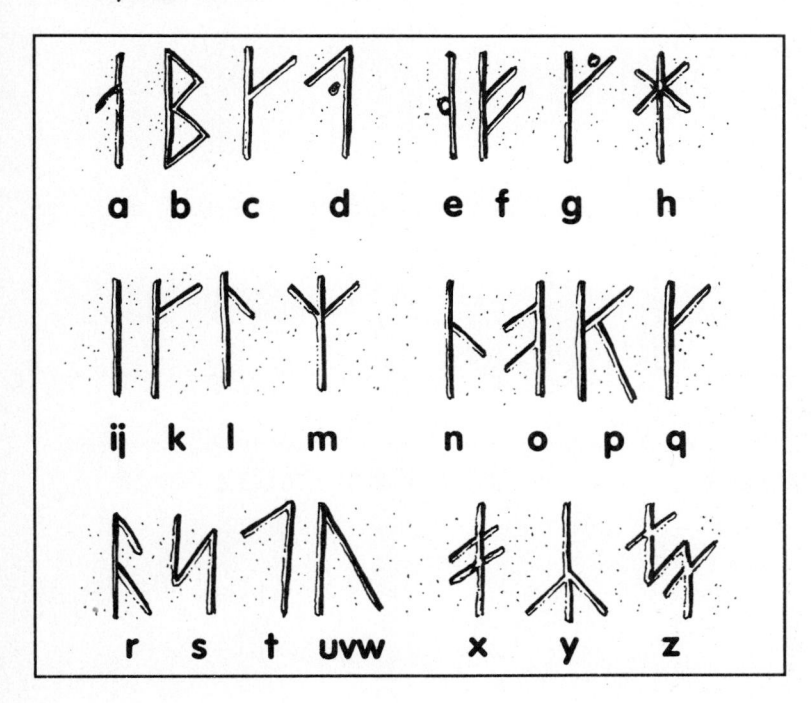

Vikings often used a snake design like this one.

♣ Write your name in runes.

♣ Draw your own snake design on the back of this page and use runes to write a secret message. Give it to a friend to read.

History

Romans, Anglo-Saxons and Vikings in Britain

Name _____

Invasion time-line

Invasion time-line

♣ Draw pictures to illustrate each event named below.
♣ The pictures are in the wrong order. Cut them out and put them in the right order to make a time-line.
♣ Can you add the dates of other important events to your time-line?

| AD250 Raids by Saxon pirates | AD43 Romans invade | AD789 First Viking raids |

| AD480 Saxon invasion | AD122 Building of Hadrian's Wall | AD161 Boudicca's revolt |

Name _____

Life in Tudor times

Planning grid

LIFE IN TUDOR TIMES

KEY QUESTIONS	CONCEPTS	CONTENT	RESOURCES, TYPES OF SOURCES	ACTIVITIES, TEACHING AND LEARNING METHODS	RECORDING AND ASSESSMENT
• Who were the kings and queens of Tudor times?	• Power • Authority	• Role of monarch today • Tudor family tree	• Drama props • Pictures of Tudor monarchs • Reference books	• Drama: symbols of monarchy • Portraites as historical source	• Participation in drama • Ability to draw meaning from pictorial sources • Ordering family tree
• What was the court of Elizabeth I like?	• Queen • Monarchy • Court • Courtiers • Chronology	• Time-line of political and economic events • Life of Elizabeth's court: food, clothes, leisure, schooling, health	• Illustrations of Tudor court • Reference books • Tudor dance music	• Discussions of duties of Queen today and in Elizabethan times • Making ruffs • Standing in portrait poses • Individual research on court themes	• Participating in discussion • Individual work on a selected Tudor topic
• What was life like outside the court?	• Rural • Urban • Inventory • Peasant • Merchant	• Farming • Markets • Town life, sanitation	• Map of Tudor Britain • Reference books • Local Tudor houses	• Teacher presentation on differences between Tudor Britain and Britain today • In pairs using resources to find out how people lived in towns and in the countryside	• Written and pictorial recording of life in Tudor Britain
• What major changes took place during Tudor times?	• Change • Empire • Exploration • Colonialism • Science • Religion	• Three Gs: God, Gold, Glory • Drake, Raleigh, Columbus • Global markets • Newton • Elizabethan theatre	• Historical atlas showing world known to Europeans in 1420, 1520 and 1650 • Reference books on Tudors • Shakespeare retold for children	• Brainstorming: local links with overseas • Teacher presentaion of world as seen by Tudors • Reflection on literature of the time • Witches as wise women – challenging stereotypes	• Understanding that there was less knowledge about the world • Recording reasons for exploration and knowledge about British explorers of the time • Awareness that lands were already settled • Questioning stereotypes

History

Life in Tudor times

Name _____

Monarchs: the two Elizabeths

Monarchs: the two Elizabeths

These two pictures show the coronation ceremonies of Elizabeth I and Elizabeth II.
✤ Look at both pictures and write down the similarities and differences between them.

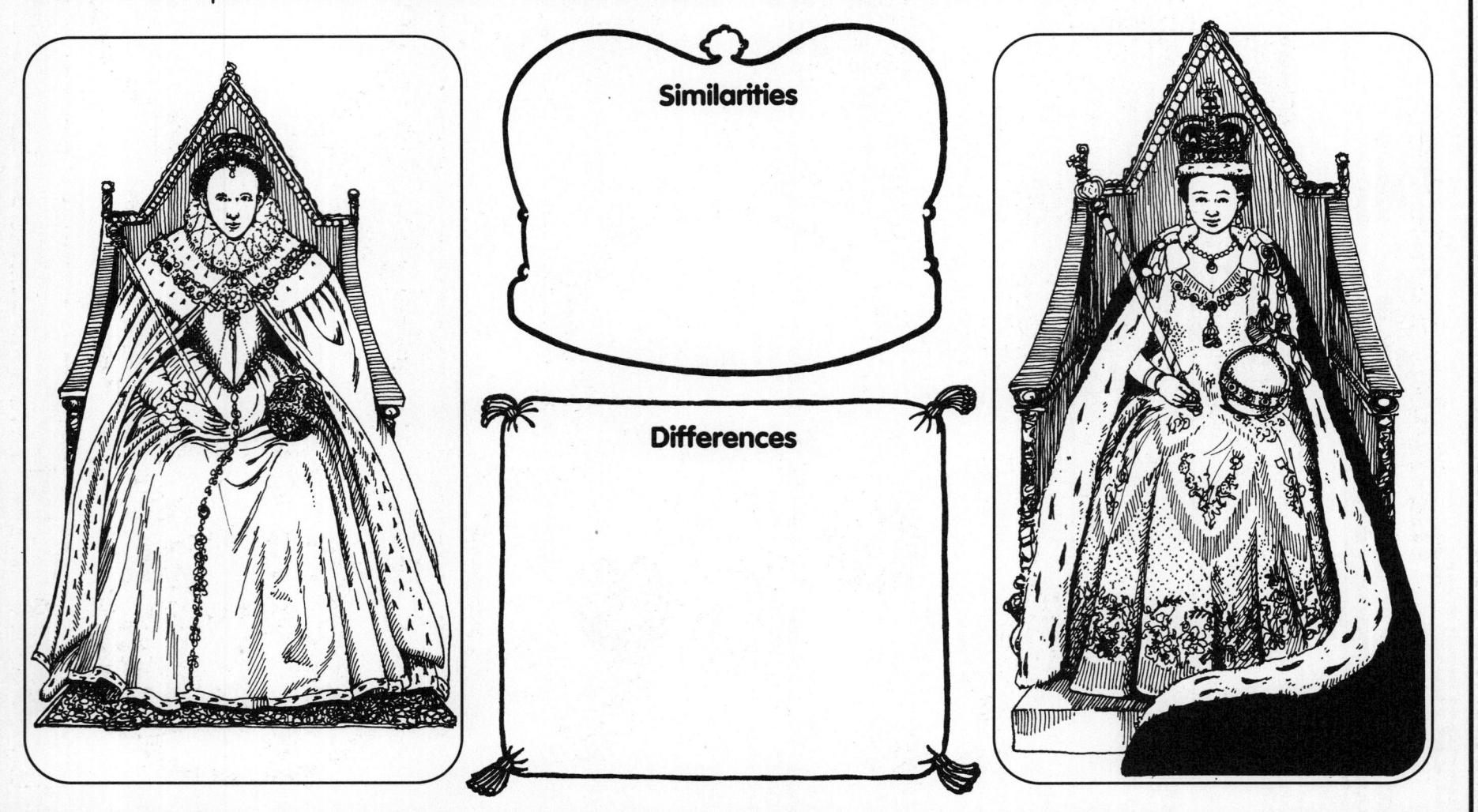

Similarities

Differences

74

History

Name _____

Life in Tudor times

The Tudor family tree

The Tudor family tree

Henry VII

Edward VI

History

75

Life in Tudor times

Name _____

The *Golden Hind*

The *Golden Hind*

In 1580 Sir Francis Drake brought the *Golden Hind*, loaded with silver and jewels taken from Spanish ships, into Plymouth. The ship had five decks and a hold below. The top deck was known as the poop deck. It held two canons. The next deck was the command deck. Below was the forecastle deck. Next down was the main deck where the officers slept. The sailors slept on the gun deck below.

♣ Label the diagram using the information given above.

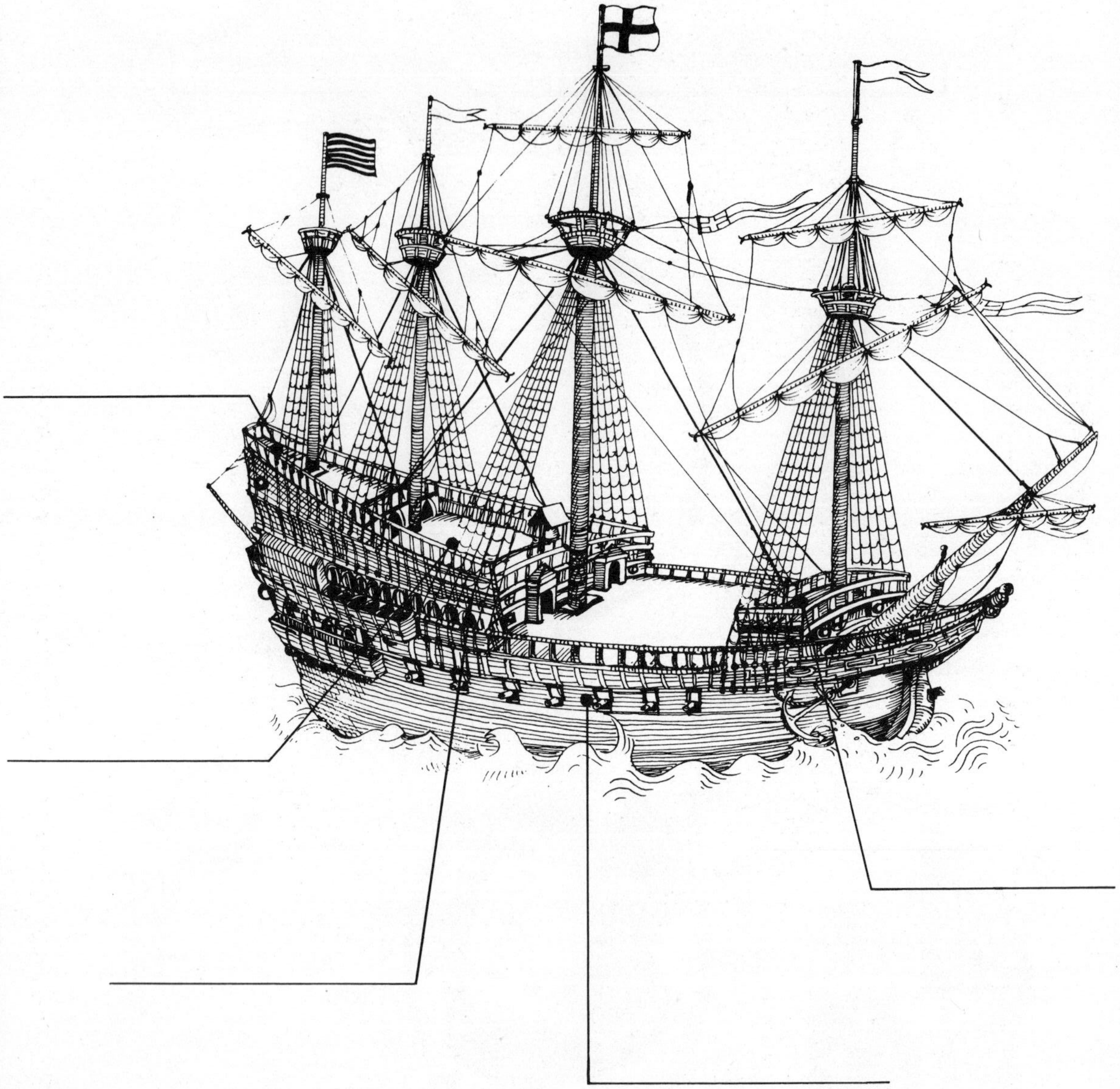

♣ Use reference books to find the answers to the following questions.
• Who was Sir Francis Drake?
• What was his most famous voyage?

76

History

Name _____

Life in Tudor times

Inventories

Inventories

When Robert Leigh of Prescot died in 1579, all his worldly possessions were valued and a list was made.

1 Cow
1 Horse
Brass and Pewter
Frying pan and other Iron
3 Pairs of Sheets
2 Coverlets
3 Carts, 1 pair of wheels
1 Collar, 2 Packsaddles
Pots
Corn and grass on the ground
Tree (wooden) ware and
1 coffer (wooden box)
Butter
Muck
Fuel
Backclothes

✤ **Complete the drawing above so that it shows some of these possessions.**

History

77

Life in Tudor times

Name _____

Women in Tudor times

Women in Tudor times

This excerpt comes from a book of advice to women about how they should act as wives.

"If you intend to be a good wife, and live comfortably, accept this. My husband is my superior and my better. He has authority and rules over me. Nature has given it to him. God has given it to him."

The Bride Bush 1617

✤ How do you know this was written a long time ago?
✤ Do you think all women took this advice?
✤ Views like this about women may have influenced Queen Elizabeth I's decision not to marry. Why?
✤ What advice would you give to women about how they should act as wives today?

History

Name _____

Life in Tudor times

Breakfast with Queen Elizabeth I

Breakfast with Queen Elizabeth I

This is an example of the food served for breakfast at Queen Elizabeth's court.

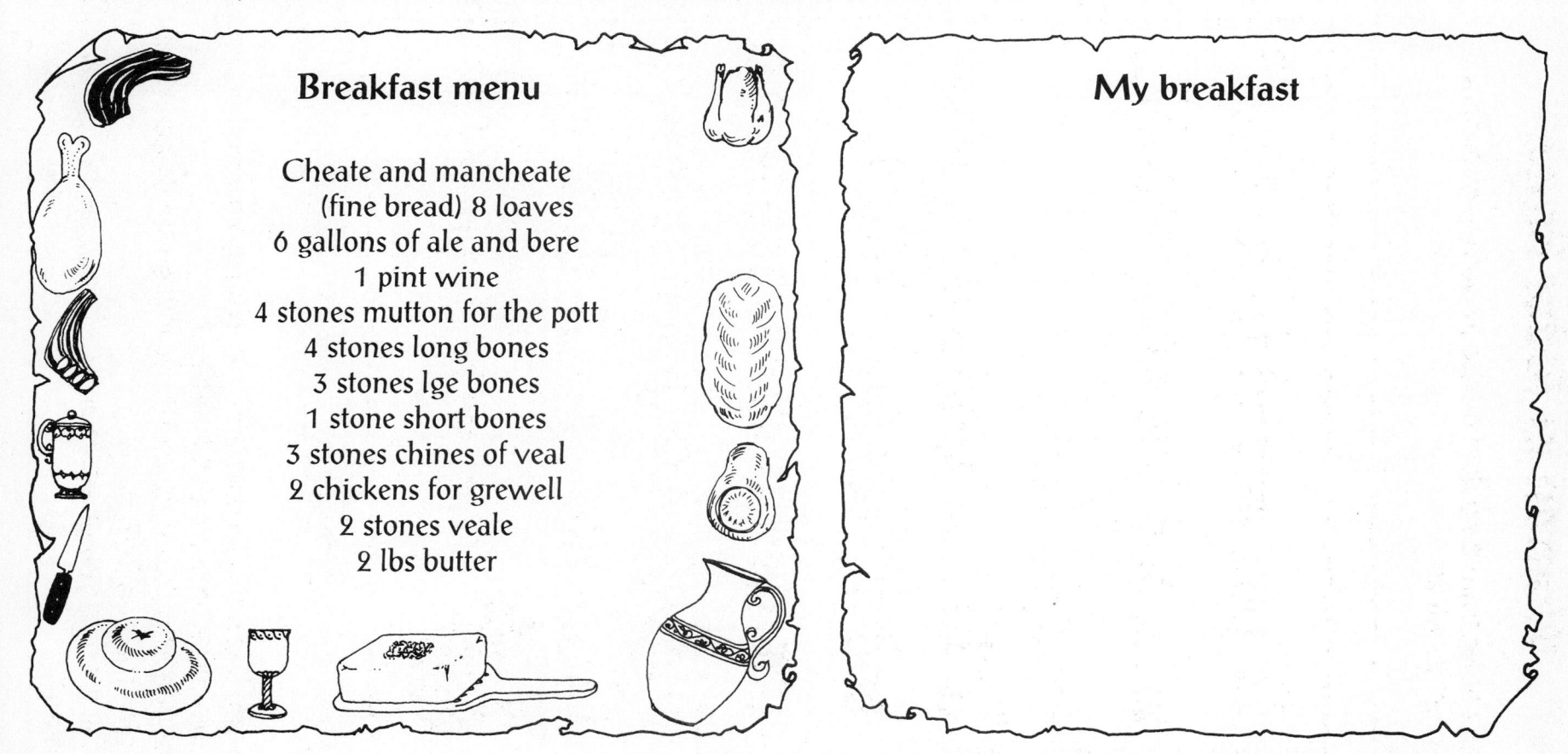

Breakfast menu

Cheate and mancheate
(fine bread) 8 loaves
6 gallons of ale and bere
1 pint wine
4 stones mutton for the pott
4 stones long bones
3 stones lge bones
1 stone short bones
3 stones chines of veal
2 chickens for grewell
2 stones veale
2 lbs butter

My breakfast

♣ List what you had for breakfast.
♣ Underline anything that is the same on both menus.
♣ Find the modern spellings of words that appear on this old menu.

History

Life in Tudor times

A Tudor kitchen

A Tudor kitchen

✤ Find some things that tell you that this is a picture of a kitchen in the past and write them here.

1 _____
2 _____
3 _____
4 _____
5 _____
6 _____
7 _____
8 _____

✤ How would the kitchen have been lit and heated?
✤ How are kitchens lit and heated today?
✤ What difference would this make to someone working in the kitchen?

History

Name _____

Life in Tudor times

Religion in Tudor times

Religion in Tudor times

England was a Catholic country at the beginning of the sixteenth century. After 1570 Catholics were persecuted.

♣ Use reference books to find out how these things changed during Tudor times:
- The inside of churches
- Monasteries
- The Bible
- The Head of the Church in England.

♣ Now find out why Elizabeth started to persecute Catholics.
♣ What might these two people be saying?

Catholics should be allowed to worship freely because ...

The Queen cannot allow Catholics to worship freely because ...

History

81

Life in Tudor times

Name _____

Elizabeth's advice to Mary Queen of Scots

Elizabeth's advice to Mary Queen of Scots

> Madam, My ears have been so astounded and my heart so frightened to hear of the horrible and abominable murder of your husband and my own cousin that I have scarcely spirit to write: yet I cannot conceal that I grieve more for you than him. I should not do the office of a faithful cousin and friend, if I did not urge you to preserve your honour, rather than look through your fingers at revenge.

Use reference books to find out more about Elizabeth and Mary Queen of Scots.
- Who was Mary's husband?
- What had happened to him?
- What advice did Elizabeth give to Mary?
- Who was Mary's son?
- What happened to Mary Queen of Scots?

Name _____

Life in Tudor times

A Tudor house

A Tudor house

This illustration shows part of a carved mantelpiece from a Tudor house. The man in the centre is William Norris. He lived from 1523 until 1568. The mantelpiece provides evidence about the Norris family.

♣ How many wives did Norris have?
♣ How many children did he have?
♣ What is the woman on his right holding? What does this tell you about the religion of the family?
♣ How old was William Norris when he died?
♣ Use reference books to find out which Tudor monarchs ruled while he was alive.

History
83

Life in Tudor times

Who's who in Tudor times?

Who's who in Tudor times?

♣ What do these Tudors have in common: Mary Queen of Scots, Lady Jane Grey, Anne Boleyn, Thomas More and Catherine Howard?

♣ What happened to these two queens: Catherine of Aragon and Anne of Cleves?

♣ Which Scottish king became King of England?

♣ Who wrote these plays: *Julius Caesar*, *Henry V* and *The Merchant of Venice*?

♣ Who sailed round the world in a ship called the *Golden Hind*?

♣ Who began the English slave trade from Sierra Leone to Hispaniola and introduced tobacco to England?

♣ Use reference books to find out more about these people.

Name _____

Victorian Britain
Planning grid

VICTORIAN BRITAIN KEY QUESTIONS	CONCEPTS	CONTENT	RESOURCES, TYPES OF SOURCES	ACTIVITIES, TEACHING AND LEARNING METHODS	RECORDING AND ASSESSMENT
• Who were the Victorians?	• Chronology	• Key dates and events during Victoria's reign	• Time-lines • Portraits of Victoria at different ages • Reference books	• Teacher presentation giving key biographical dates for Victoria to start class time-line (added to as unit progresses) • Individual time-lines • Famous Victorians time-line	• Can the children sequence events correctly? • Can they explain why this period is called 'the Victorian age'?
• What was life like in Victorian Britain?	• Wealth • Poverty • Class	• Housing • Family life • Gender roles • Transport • Leisure • Work • Education • Religion	• Reference books • Photographs and illustrations • Written sources (directories, newspaper extracts, adverts) • Artefacts • Museums • Victorian 'recreations' • Buildings in locality • Victorian music • Historical fiction	• Research into different aspects of life using a range of sources • Individual, pair or group work over period of time, class display • Adopting a Victorian identity and writing an autobiography • Creating a Victorian parlour in the classroom • Holding a Victorian day	• Can pupils describe the daily life of a rich family and a poor family? • Can they extract and transfer information from a range of sources?
• Where were the most important changes and how did these effect people?	• Industry • Trade • Public health • Transport • Emigration • Inventions	• Growth of industry • Working conditions • Child labour • Women workers • Growth of towns: reasons and results • Reforms in labour, public health and education • Public buildings • Growth of railways • Movements of people • Developments in different areas (e.g. leisure, medicine, science, technology)	• Reference books • Photographs and illustrations • Written sources • Artefacts • Museums • Buildings • Maps and atlases • Historical fiction • Time-line • Victorian town plans	• Variety of research activities and teacher presentations • Local sources used initially before wider perspective • Comparing size of towns at start and end of Victoria's rule • Identifying reasons for growth and its results • Investigating the conditions of working women and children • Identifying the living conditions that made public health reforms necessary • A time-line of major reforms • Researching Victorian inventions of everyday items and their impact • A time-line of inventions	• Can the children extract and transfer information from a range of sources? • Can they identify some of the positive aspects of the Victorian era, as well as the negative ones?
• What was Britain's influence on the rest of the world?	• Trade • Empire • Exploration • Emigration • Exploration	• Goods imported and exported • Countries with which GB traded • Famous explorers • Countries of Empire and its effects • Reasons for emigration	• Atlases • Large-scale maps • Reference books • Pictures and photos	• Identification on map of areas conquered and of the extent of empire • Discussing impact of the Empire • Using sources to discover Victorian attitude to Empire	• Can children identify some of the countries of the Empire? • Can they describe the benefits and disadvantages of being part of the Empire?

History

85

Victorian Britain

Name _____

Victorian time-line

The pictures show some of the important events during the 63 years of Queen Victoria's rule.
♣ Fill in the missing dates. Cut out the pictures and put them in order to make a time-line.

Date: _____

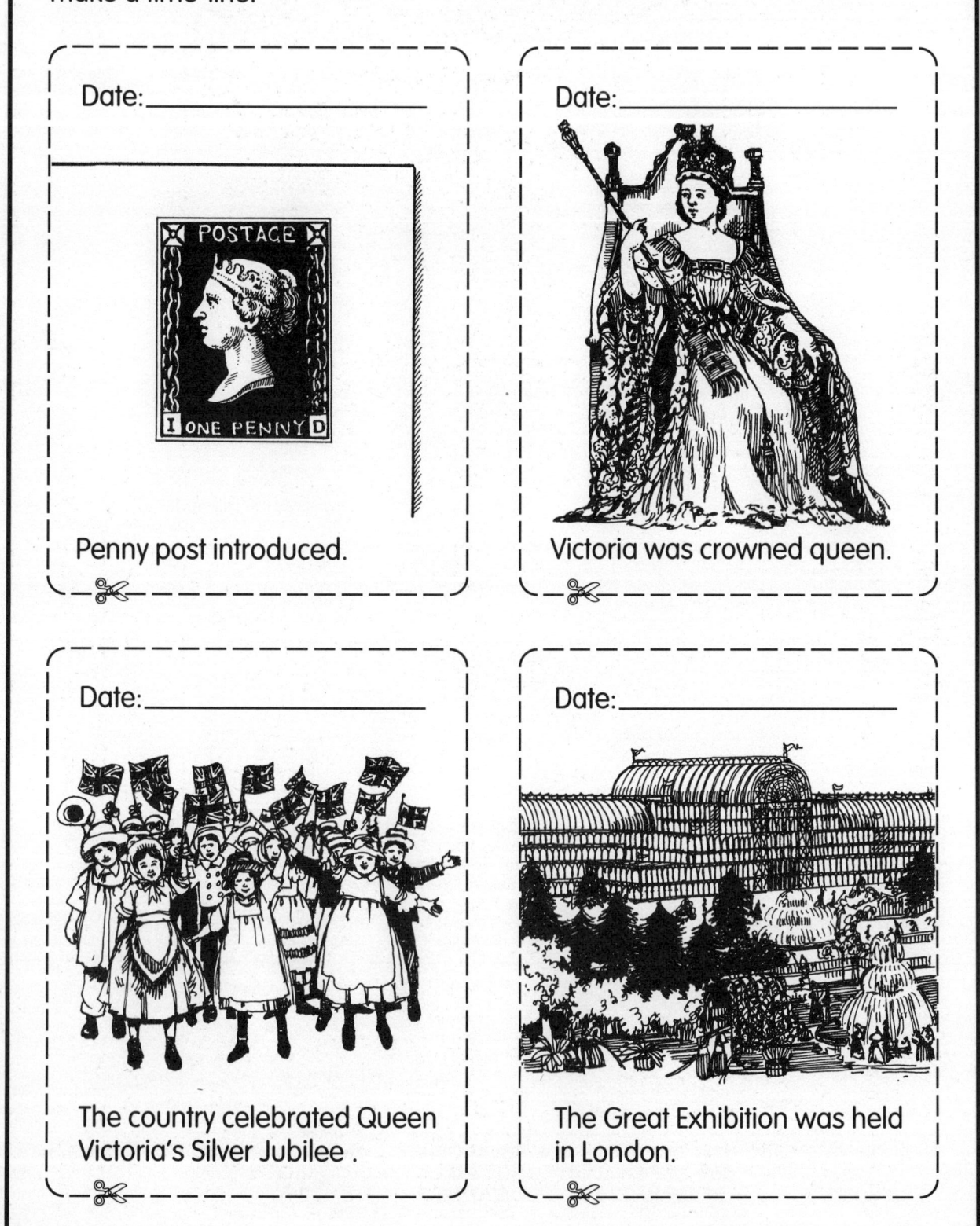

Victoria was crowned queen.

Date: _____

The Great Exhibition was held in London.

Date: _____

Penny post introduced.

Date: _____

The country celebrated Queen Victoria's Silver Jubilee.

86

History

Name _____

Victorian Britain

Victorian families

Victorian families

♣ The pictures show two Victorian families. Look at them carefully.

♣ Describe each family. Which one is richer? How can you tell?
♣ Can you find anything that is the same in both pictures?
♣ Find out more about the life of the rich and the poor in Victorian times.

History

87

Victorian Britain

Court dwellings

Poor housing was a cause for concern during Victoria's reign. This plan was drawn in 1845 for the Royal Commission on the State of the Large Towns. It shows a typical 'court' in Nottingham.

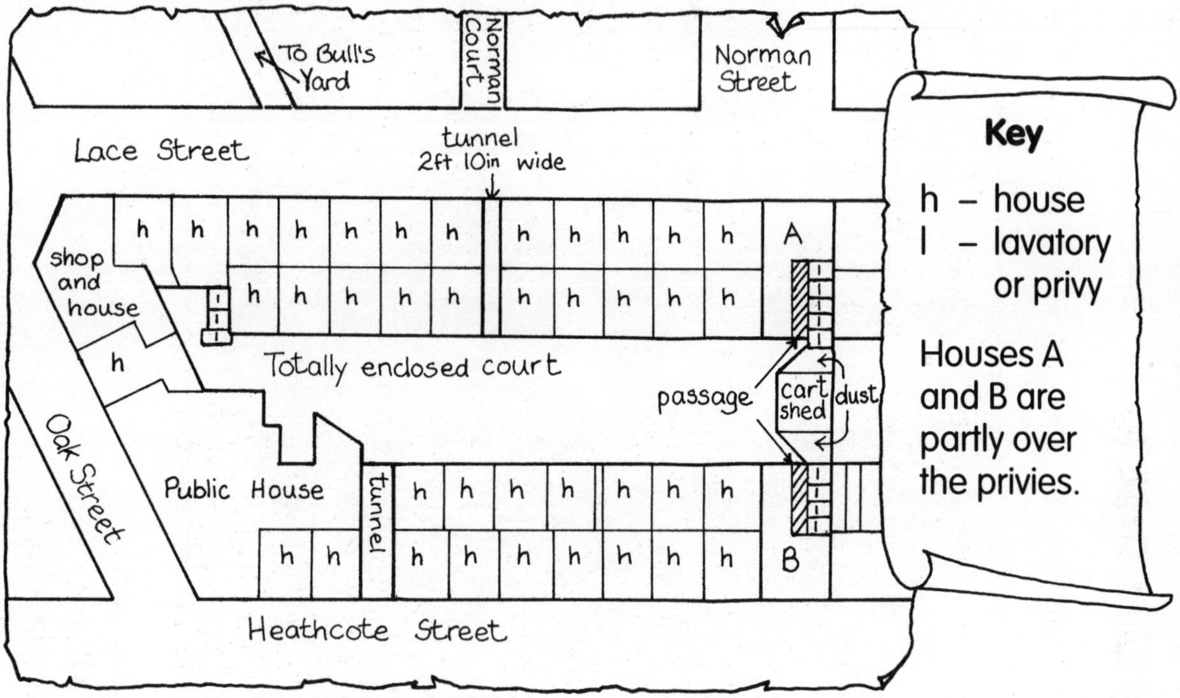

Key
h – house
l – lavatory or privy

Houses A and B are partly over the privies.

♣ List the effects of such housing on the inhabitants.

Description	Effects on inhabitants
Houses built round a narrow 'court'.	
Open drain running through the court.	
Families often had five or more members.	
Some rooms had no windows.	
Water came from a single tap in the court.	

88 History

Name _____

Victorian Britain

Home sweet home

Home sweet home

Many Victorian families lived in poor conditions. The picture and extracts describe one family's home in London in 1854.

> The room is little more than 7 feet long by 6 feet wide; the greatest height 6 feet 9 inches. The narrow bedstead, which is doubled up in the daytime, reaches, when let down, close to the fireplace.

> The roof and part of the wall are mildewed with damp; through parts of the roof the sky is distinctly visible. The room is occupied by a married couple of about 22 or 23 years of age, and a little girl about 2 years old.

❖ Use the picture and the descriptions to draw a plan of the room.
❖ What would be the effects on the family of living in this home?
❖ Why do you think many families had to live in conditions like this?

History

Victorian Britain

Victorian holidays

Name _____

Victorian holidays

This illustration shows a wealthy Victorian family preparing for their holiday.

♣ Say who the people in the picture are. Describe their appearance and clothes.
♣ Tell the story of what is happening in the picture.
♣ Compare your story with a friend's. Are they the same?

Name _____

Victorian Britain

Children at work

Children at work

In Victorian times many children worked. The illustrations show child workers.

Factory worker   **Cress-seller**   **Farm labourer**   **Brickworker**

✤ Which of these occupations would you choose to do? Give the reasons for your choice. Describe your work.
✤ Why did so many Victorian children have to work? What were the effects on the children? Do you think child labour was a good thing or not?
✤ Find other kinds of work carried out by children during Queen Victoria's reign.
✤ Using the back of this page, make a list of the kinds of work that children do nowadays.

Victorian Britain

Workhouse children

Workhouse children

The workhouse provided a place of shelter for old people who could not work and for the families of workers who were unemployed. Conditions inside the workhouse were very harsh. Children were separated from their parents. The two sources below give an idea of what it was like to be a workhouse child.

FOR CHILDREN UNDER 9 YEARS OF AGE

Breakfast
Bread and milk porridge as normal

Dinner
Suet pudding three times a week
Cooked meat with veg and bread twice a week
Coffee with bread and butter twice a week

Supper
Milk porridge for those over 4 years of age, and for those under 4 years of age a sufficient quantity of bread and new milk

Bolton Chronicle 16 March 1853

♣ The extract shows what a child had to eat each day. Do you think this diet would be enough for the children? What kinds of food are missing from the workhouse diet?
♣ List everything you ate yesterday and compare it with what a workhouse child would eat in one day.
♣ Use the illustration to describe the clothes and appearance of a workhouse child.

Name _____

Victorian Britain

Victorian women

Victorian women

The illustrations show some examples of working women in Queen Victoria's time.

Servant   **Factory worker**   **Coster-woman**   **Pit-brow lass**

✤ Describe what each job involved. Why do you think women went out to work?
✤ Find other types of work done by Victorian women.
✤ Make a list of different kinds of work that women do today.

History

93

Victorian Britain

King Cholera

Name _____

King Cholera

Cholera is a deadly disease. In 1849 over 50,000 people died from cholera in England and Wales. It was called 'King Cholera' because it affected rich people as well as the poor. Little was known about the reasons for its outbreak. Here are three examples of evidence about cholera.

'The first case was that of Joseph Crosby residing in Mechanic Street, in a confined yard 13 feet by 15 feet long into which one other house opens and two others abut, leaving only a three foot passage without any through ventilation. The house in question presents dirty walls and ceiling, the floor partly covered with broken flags, the remaining portion being unflagged; no ventilation from windows, an offensive drain in the yard alluded to.'

(Report by Inspector of Nuisances 9 Sept 1854)

'Advice during the visitation of the cholera:
• Beware of drink; for excess in beer, wine or spirits is likely to be followed by cholera.
• Avoid eating meat that is tainted or unwholesome, decayed or unripe fruit and stale fish and vegetables.
• Avoid fasting too long. Be moderate at meals.
• Avoid great fatigue or getting heated and then chilled.
• Avoid getting wet or remaining in wet clothing.'

(Bolton Chronicle 9 September 1854)

♣ What does each of these examples tell us about what people thought were the causes of cholera?
♣ Which is the most useful piece of evidence? Why?

Name _____

Victorian Britain

Inventions of the Victorian era

Inventions of the Victorian era

Many things that we take for granted today were invented during Queen Victoria's reign. Here are some examples.

Electric light bulb
1879

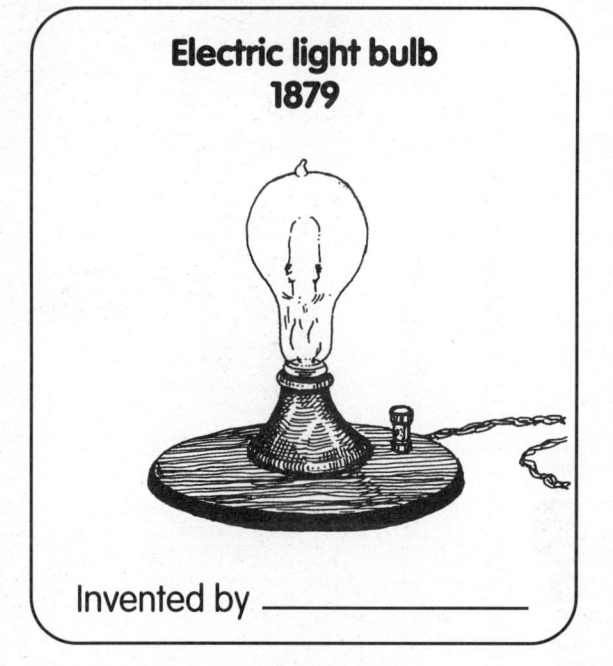

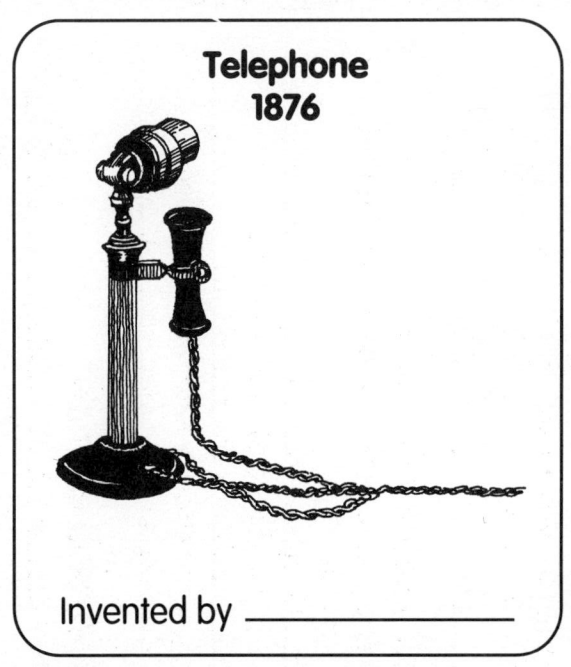

Invented by _____

Gramophone
1877

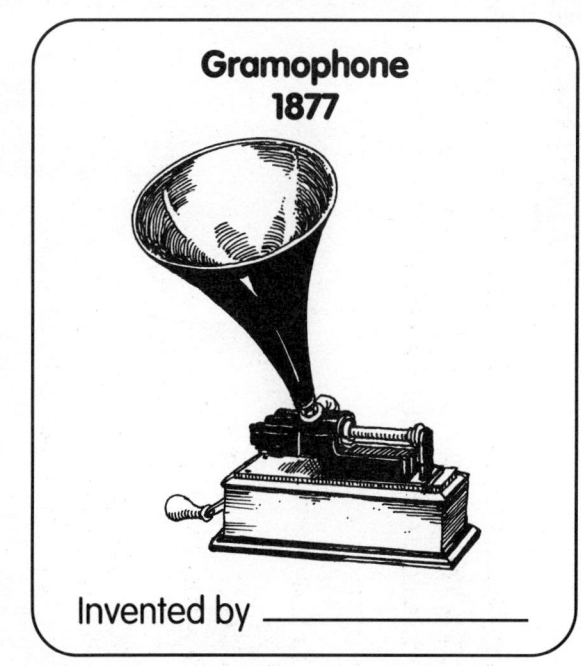

Invented by _____

Petrol-driven car
1885

Invented by _____

Telephone
1876

Invented by _____

♣ Find out the name of each inventor and write it down.
♣ Explain why each invention was important and describe the effect it had on people's lives.
♣ Find out about one or two other things invented during Victoria's reign.

History

95

Victorian Britain

Famous Victorians

Name _____

Famous Victorians

The portraits show four people who were famous during Queen Victoria's reign and who are still remembered today.
♣ Use reference books to find out why each one is famous and write it beneath each picture.

Elizabeth Fry    **Charles Dickens**    **Mrs Beeton**    **Isambard K. Brunel**

_____   _____   _____   _____
_____   _____   _____   _____
_____   _____   _____   _____

♣ Now choose two more examples of famous Victorians. Using the back of this page, draw their pictures and write about why they were famous.

History

Name _____

Britain since 1930

Planning grid

BRITAIN SINCE 1930

KEY QUESTIONS	CONCEPTS	CONTENT	RESOURCES, TYPES OF SOURCES	ACTIVITIES, TEACHING AND LEARNING METHODS	RECORDING AND ASSESSMENT
Approach A (by decade) • How did people live during the 1930s, 40s, 50s, 60s, 70s, 80s? (or taken in reverse order)	• Decade • Stereotyping • Bias • Interpretation • Historian • Evidence • Immigration • Emigration • Chronology	• Use of primary sources to find out what life was like in a given decade • Defining criteria for examining evidence from the past • Creating a time-line of political events • Creating a social events time-line	• Oral histories • Photographs and other visual material • Artefacts including household objects, commemorative china, coins and stamps • Written sources including local newspapers • Reference books • Buildings • Use of local area	• Collection and display of evidence about specific decades • Classification and interpretation of evidence • Looking at bias in evidence • Writing up findings into decades books	• Interest in and awareness of primary source material • Ability to interpret evidence • Recording methodology and findings in relation to evidence
Approach B (by theme) • How have employment, industry, transport, housing, leisure, religion, family life changed since 1930? (or taken in reverse order)	• Change • Continuity • Cause • Culture • Reaction • Immigration • Emigration • Chronology	• Use of primary and secondary sources on specific aspects of life to show change and continuity over the last sixty years	• As above	• Teacher presentation on researching aspects of social history over a period of time, using one particular aspect as an example • Individual research on topics using primary and secondary sources • Group/class presentation	• Ability to use information from teacher • Presentation as framework for own subject matter • Enthusiasm in researching individual topics • Ability to use materials provided and to search out others • Clarity in expression of ideas and presentation
• How did the Second World War effect people in Britain?	• War • Evacuation • Dictator • Fascism • Propaganda • Nation • Holocaust • Conscientious objectors • Home front • Chronology	• Using primary and secondary sources to show preparation for hostilities • Overview of events of war • Wartime Britain for children and adults	• Primary and secondary sources (as above) • World maps • Historical atlas • Use of local and national newspapers and other written sources	• Teacher presentation providing overview of build-up to World War II • Major events as they affected the home population • Individual research using primary and secondary sources to show life during World War II in the local area • Teacher presentation on wars as ongoing events (Cold War, Falklands War, Northern Ireland, wars of independence, etc.)	• Progression in abilities to use primary and secondary sources to provide a history of the past • Maturity in interpretation of evidence • Response to request for primary and secondary sources

• Both approaches require an examination of the impact of World War II.

History

97

Britain since 1930

Name _____

Key events time-line

Key events time-line

♣ Use a variety of historical sources to complete this time-line.

Decade	Events
1930s	
1940s	
1950s	
1960s	
1970s	
1980s	
1990s	

♣ How did you decide which events to include?

98

History

Name _____

Britain since 1930

The Holocaust

The Holocaust

The following evidence was given by Rudolf Hoess, Commandant of Auschwitz, at the Nuremberg war crimes trial.

'I was ordered to establish extermination facilities at Auschwitz. I visited Treblinka (another concentration camp) to find out how they carried out exterminations. The commandant told me he had liquified 80,000 in one half year....It took from three to fifteen minutes to kill people. We knew when they were dead because their screaming stopped. After the bodies were removed, our special commandos took off the rings and extracted the gold from the teeth of the corpses...we built our gas chambers to take 2,000 people at a time.'

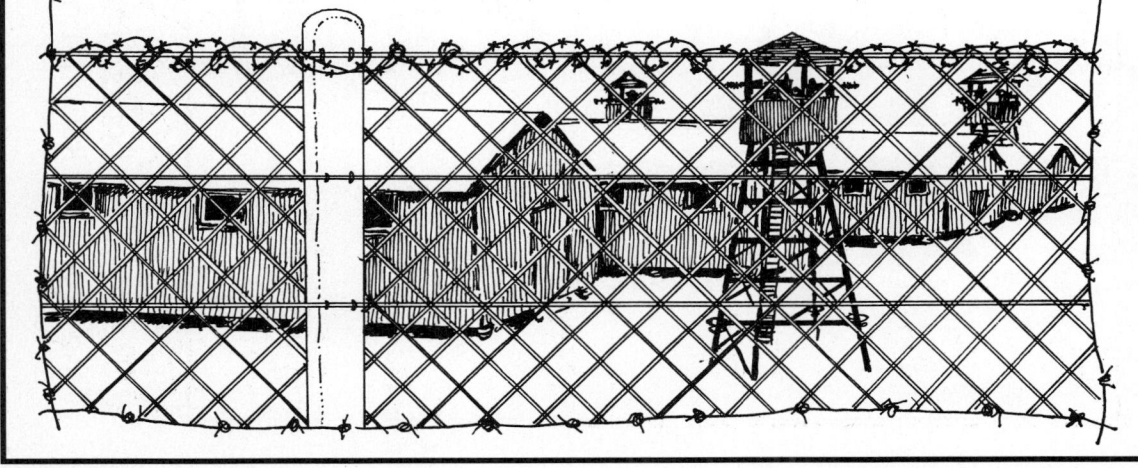

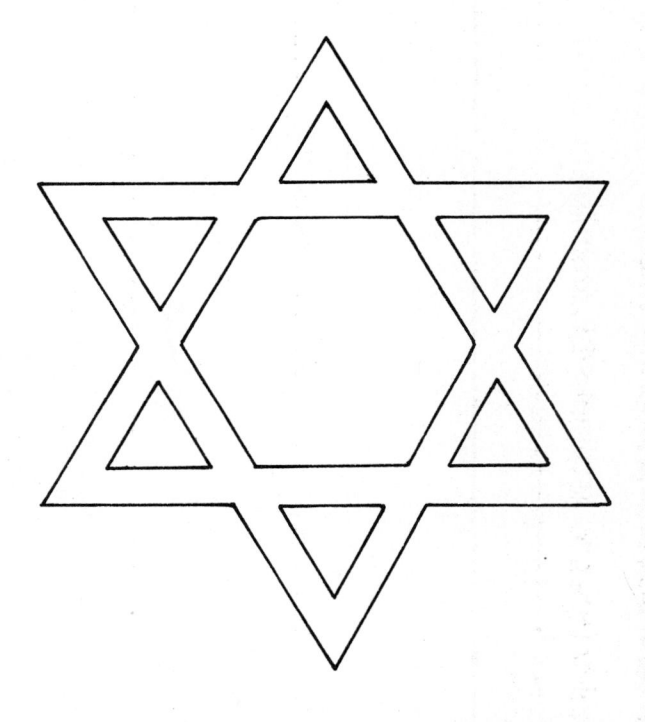

♣ Use reference books to find out about the Holocaust.
♣ Using the back of this sheet, write down what happened and when it happened. Why is it important that these events are remembered?
♣ The illustration above shows the Star of David, a symbol of the Jewish people. Find out about its history.

Britain since 1930

Name _____

Nazi education

Nazi education

This illustration is like those in German children's books in the Nazi era.
♣ Write down what you think the picture is saying.

♣ Use reference books to find the names of some of the leading members of the Nazi party in Germany.

100

History

Name _____

Britain since 1930

The Blitz

The Blitz

Source 1

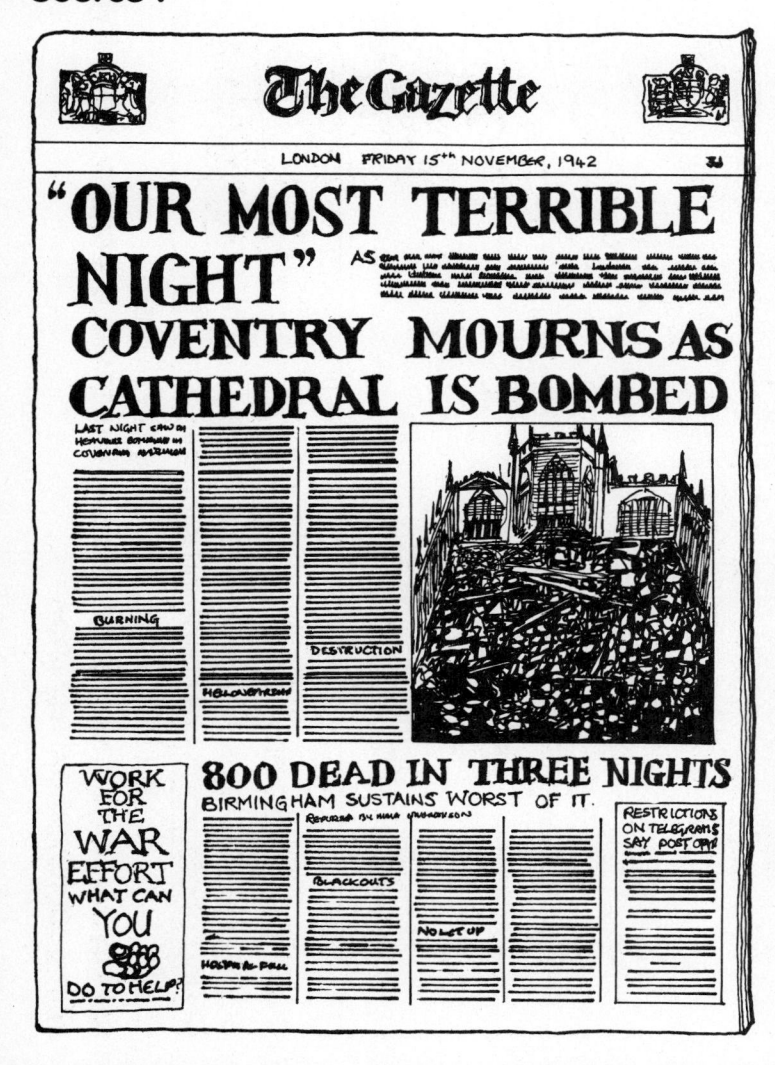

The Gazette

LONDON FRIDAY 15th NOVEMBER, 1942

"OUR MOST TERRIBLE NIGHT"
COVENTRY MOURNS AS CATHEDRAL IS BOMBED

800 DEAD IN THREE NIGHTS
BIRMINGHAM SUSTAINS WORST OF IT.

WORK FOR THE WAR EFFORT WHAT CAN YOU DO TO HELP?

Source 2

'The house lay on the Nazi air route to the Midlands, now known as "Hell's Corridor"; when the raids spread north and west of London, the hours of darkness became more clamorous. On November 14th, the night of the great attack on Coventry, the sky hummed for four hours like a hive of gigantic bees; from dark to dawn the barrage flashed all round the horizon. Pulling aside by my black-out curtains, I watched for an hour the anti-aircraft shells bursting ineffectively beneath the unseen raiders....800 people in Birmingham were killed and 2,000 injured on three successive nights.'

Vera Brittain, writer and campaigner

♣ Use reference books and other historical sources to collect more evidence about the Blitz. How did people try to protect themselves?

♣ Make a list below of some of the most heavily bombed towns. On the back of this sheet, write down why you think these particular towns were so heavily bombed.

History

Britain since 1930

Name _____

Evacuation

Evacuation

Ann was three when she was evacuated from Liverpool to Southport in 1940. This is what she took with her.

♣ What do these objects tell us about Ann?
♣ Why do you think her mother put in the cake mix?
♣ Find photographs of children being evacuated.
♣ What would you take if you had to leave home?
♣ How would you feel about leaving home with a single suitcase to live with people you did not know?

102

History

Name _____

Britain since 1930

Wartime persuasion: evacuation

Wartime persuasion: evacuation

TAKE THEM BACK! TAKE THEM BACK!... TAKE THEM BACK!

DON'T do it, Mother —

LEAVE THE CHILDREN WHERE THEY ARE

ISSUED BY THE MINISTRY OF HEALTH

♣ What message does this poster give? Why is it addressed to mothers? Why do you think the designer of the poster made Hitler into a faint outline?
♣ Find other wartime posters.
♣ Ask someone over 60 what they remember about wartime propaganda.

History

103

Britain since 1930

Name _____

Staying at home

Staying at home

Michael Foreman, author and illustrator, has written about his war experiences in Lowestoft, where his mother ran a shop. This is an extract from his book, *War Boy*.

'We had no garden. The tiny yard at the back was filled with sacks of potatoes, carrots and turnips. Even our big tin bath on the coal bunker was full of cabbages and cauliflowers from one Saturday night to the next.

'The shop, then, was the playground of my toddler years. That the shop was perpetually full of soldiers and sailors seemed quite normal to me. In 1940 the whole world seemed full of soldiers and sailors.'

♣ What information does this extract give us about the author's life in wartime Britain?
♣ Find Lowestoft on a map. Discuss why you think it was a front-line target throughout the war.
♣ Why do you think Michael was not evacuated?
♣ Draw Michael's backyard.

Name _____

Britain since 1930

Identity cards for the under-sixteens

Identity cards for the under-sixteens

NATIONAL REGISTRATION

IDENTITY CARD

UNDER SIXTEEN YEARS

NUMBER		SURNAME
WNGL 4OY:—		BLAKE

CHRISTIAN NAMES (first only in full)
JOHN D.

FULL POSTAL ADDRESS
2 CROFT ROAD
Kentish Town, London NW

THIS IDENTITY CARD IS VALID UNTIL
July 15th 19 44 ONLY

Stamp: NATIONAL REGISTRATION OFFICE 2 OCT 1939

CHANGES OF ADDRESS. No entry except by National Registration Officer, to whom removal must be notified.

REMOVED TO (Full Postal Address)
'Longford Farm', Overdale, Yorkshire

Stamp: NATIONAL REGISTRATION OFFICE 1 NOV 1939

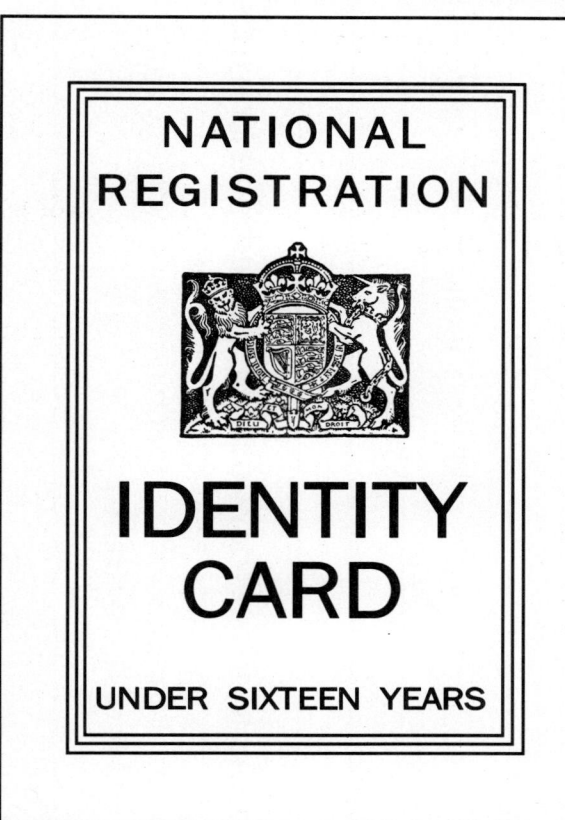

REMOVED TO (Full Postal Address)

REMOVED TO (Full Postal Address)

REMOVED TO (Full Postal Address)

♣ Say to whom this card belonged. How old was the holder of the card?
♣ How old would he or she be today?
♣ What other information does this card provide?
♣ What additional evidence does it provide?
♣ Make your own identity card.

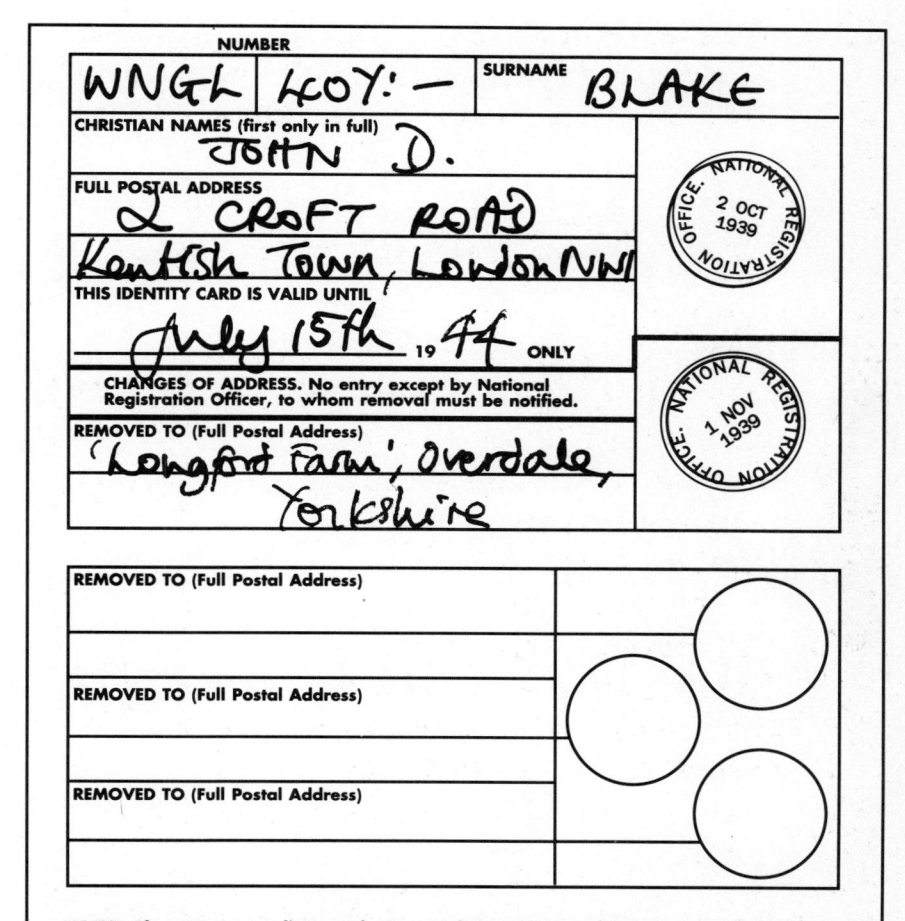

NOTICE. The parent, guardian or other person having charge of the person to whom this Card relates must sign his or her name in the first vacant space on the back.

The person having charge is responsible for the custody and production, when required, of this Identity Card and for the notification of any change of address of the person to whom it relates.

Within seven days after the 16th birthday of the person to whom this card relates that person must produce it at the local National Registration Office for the issue of a new Card.

Britain since 1930

Rationing

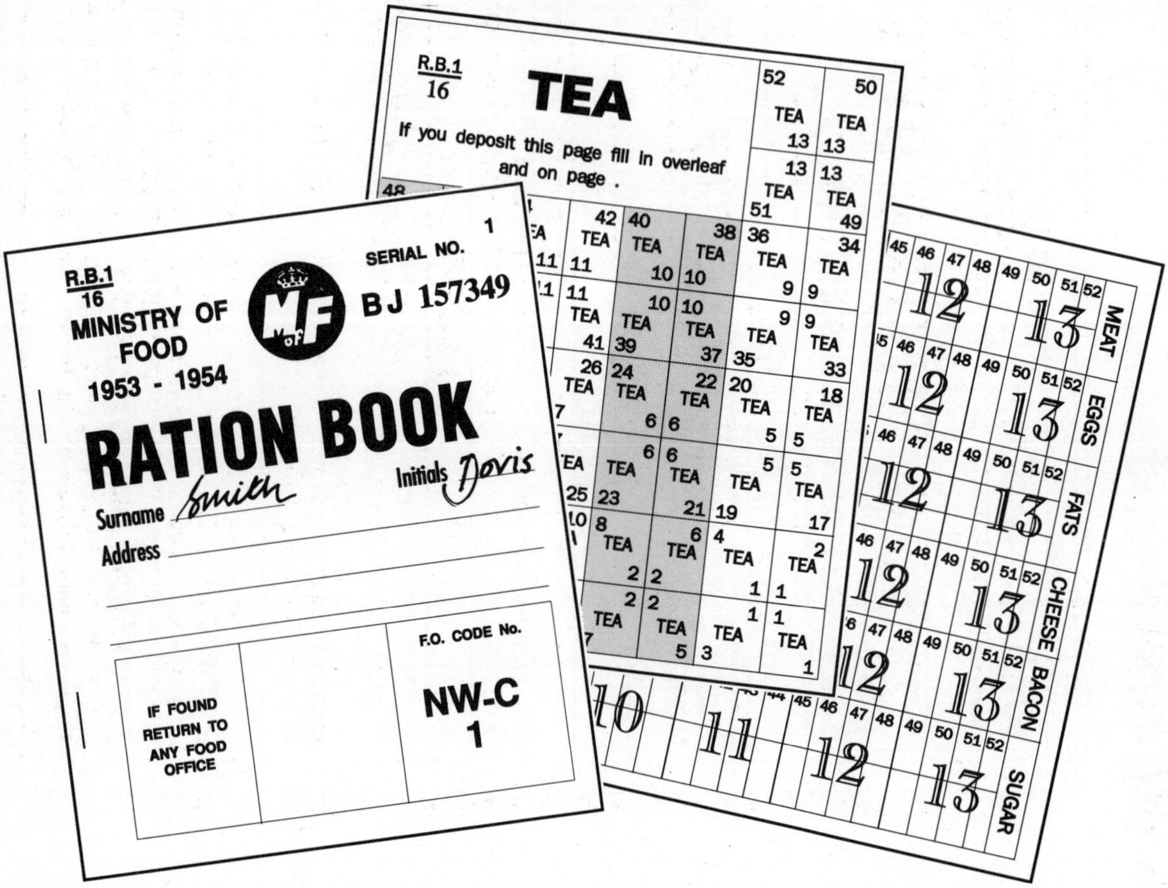

♣ Can you say what information this written source provides? Why do you think ration books were needed?

♣ Find a real ration book and note its additional features, such as colour, texture and size.

♣ Use reference books to find out how rationing worked, how long it lasted and how many coupons were needed for everyday items.
♣ Ask someone who remembers about rationing how it worked. Write down a summary of his or her evidence.

♣ Compare the different sources of evidence you have found.

Name _____

Britain since 1930

The armed forces

The armed forces

Women formed an important part of the armed forces.

♣ What information do the two written sources shown here provide?

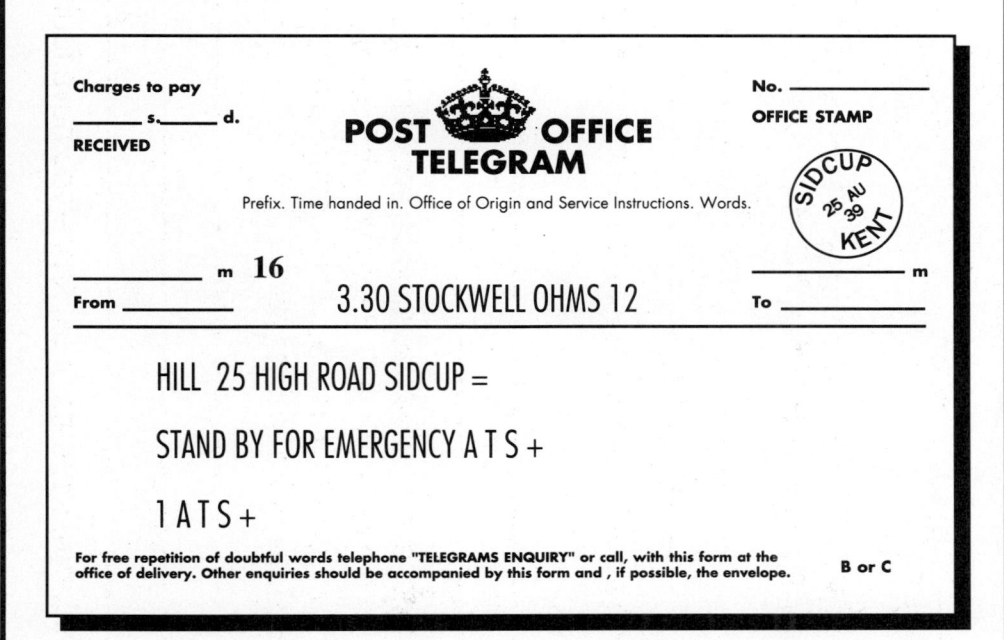

POST OFFICE TELEGRAM

Charges to pay ___ s. ___ d.
RECEIVED

No. _____
OFFICE STAMP

SIDCUP 25 AU 39 KENT

Prefix. Time handed in. Office of Origin and Service Instructions. Words.

___ m 16 3.30 STOCKWELL OHMS 12 To ___ m
From

HILL 25 HIGH ROAD SIDCUP =

STAND BY FOR EMERGENCY A T S +

1 ATS +

For free repetition of doubtful words telephone "TELEGRAMS ENQUIRY" or call, with this form at the office of delivery. Other enquiries should be accompanied by this form and, if possible, the envelope.

B or C

No. W/17021   Army Form E. 511H

CALLING UP NOTICE TO BE SENT TO EACH OFFICER AND MEMBER OF THE AUXILIARY TERRITORIAL SERVICE ON AN EMERGENCY ARISING.

AUXILIARY TERRITORIAL SERVICE
NOTICE TO JOIN

Surname __HILL__

Christian names __BETTY MARGARET (Miss)__

Address __25 HIGH ROAD__
__SIDCUP__

In accordance with the conditions of your enrolment you are hereby required to present yourself at the Headquarters of your Company __23rd Co. of London__

You should therefore report at __43 Eltham Road, Lee Green__

on __Sat. 26.8.39__ not later than __3pm__ o'clock bringing this notice with you.

If your Health Insurance Contribution Card and/or Unemployment Book are in the possession of your employer or of the Employment Exchange, you should obtain them, if possible, and bring them with you. But IF YOU ARE UNABLE TO GET THEM YOU MUST NOT DELAY JOINING ON THIS ACCOUNT. If you have to apply to the Employment Exchange for your Unemployment Book, you should take with you the Receipt Card (U.I.40) and this notice

---

♣ Interview someone who served in the Auxiliary Territorial Service and find out the sort of work they did.

♣ Make a collection of photographs or illustrations which show women in the armed forces during World War II.

Britain since 1930

At sea

At sea

The following excerpts come from a recording made by Norman Jones, a former sailor in the Royal Navy. He joined the Navy when he was 15, served during the war and then rejoined the Navy after the war.

'A sight I'll never forget was an ammunitions ship going up. It just disintegrated before your eyes.'

'The worse sound I ever heard were the depth charges at night-time. When you were escorting a convoy you could hear the charges and you knew submarines were around.'

'The best time was when you heard "This ship is bound for the UK" over the ship's Tannoy.'

♣ There are several technical terms here – convoy, depth charges, submarine, ammunitions and Tannoy. Use reference books to find out what they mean.
♣ Why do you think many people wanted to rejoin the armed forces when the war was over? Find someone who did this who will be able to help you answer the question.
♣ Why do you think people join the armed forces today?

Name _____

Ancient Greece
Planning grid

ANCIENT GREECE					
KEY QUESTIONS	**CONCEPTS**	**CONTENT**	**RESOURCES, TYPES OF SOURCES**	**ACTIVITIES, TEACHING AND LEARNING METHODS**	**RECORDING AND ASSESSMENT**
• Who were the ancient Greeks?	• Chronology in myths and legends, and in relation to ancient historical time	• Story of Troy and Odysseus • Homer's recording of this story in 900BC • Making relevant connections between Greece then and now	• Atlas • Time-line • Books on Greek myths and legends	• Reading or telling story of the fall of Troy and of Odysseus • Using world map to look up the UK and nearest town to school and to look up Greece • Using map to find Troy and Ithaca • Making a time-line	• Ability to retell story • Locating and transferring information from atlas and story-books to maps and relating modern map to the ancient one • Understanding chronology
• How do we find out about them?	• Classification of different types of evidence: archaeological, literary, numismatic, epigraphic • Interpretation of evidence • Chronology	• Herodotus the father of history and the story of Marathon • Research projects on sport, famous Greeks, art, coins, drama, literature	• Map of ancient Greece • Reference books • Travel brochures • Postcards, photographs and paintings showing evidence of life in ancient Greece • Links (if any) with nearest museum	• Teacher presentation on Herodotus and Marathon • Using time-line and maps to locate time and place of events • Using evidence from reference books, postcards and photos to find out more about sport, famous Greeks, art and coins	• Locating Marathon on map of Ancient Greece • Sequencing a story • Ability to use evidence provided to give oral, pictorial or written account of how evidence informs us about the past • Ability to complete assigned worksheets
• How were children educated?	• Citizenship • Democracy • Similarities and differences between past and present	• Learning to be a citizen today and in ancient Greece • Differences between schools now and then • Differences between schooling in Sparta and Athens • Continued work on resource project	• Reference books • Map of ancient Greece • Greek alphabet	• Discussion of purposes of education today and in Ancient Greece • Rights and duties of citizenship • Greeks' perception of education for boys and girls and for slaves • Writing own names and secret messages in Greek alphabet • Continuing own resource project	• Participation and understanding of key issues involved in discussion • Location of Athens and Sparta on map • Ability to use referencing skills
• How did people live in ancient Greece?	• Farming • Peasants • Economy • Trade • Colony • Empire	• Farming in Greece • Types of land • Main crops • Importance of olives • Ships and shipping	• Travel brochures • Map of world • Map of ancient Greece • Postcards, photographs, illustrations from reference books • Jar of olives • Olive oil	• Identifying types of land from travel brochures and reference books (in pairs) • Investigating farming now and then • Uses of olive oil now and then • Researching trade growth of Greece • Merchant ships and warships	• Recording types of land in Ancient Greece • Ability to see continuity between past and present • Use of referencing skills

Ancient Greece

Name _____

Greece today

Greece today

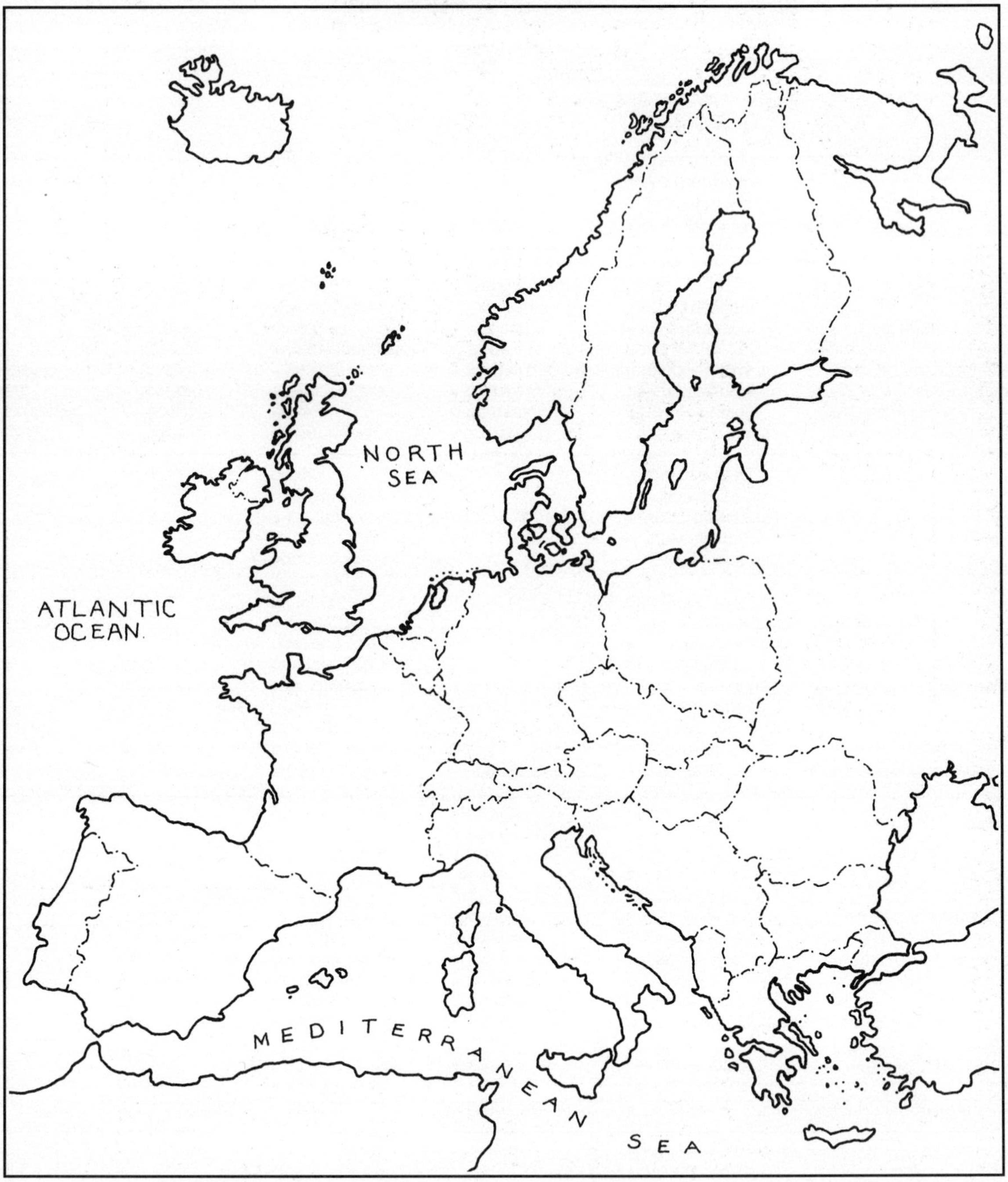

NORTH SEA

MEDITERRANEAN SEA

ATLANTIC OCEAN

♣ Put a circle round the United Kingdom. Mark with a dot the nearest large town to your school.
♣ Use an atlas to find Greece. Now circle Greece on this map. Which continent is it in?
♣ Use reference books to find out more about Greece today.
♣ Using the back of this page, write down three questions about Greece for a friend to answer.

110   History

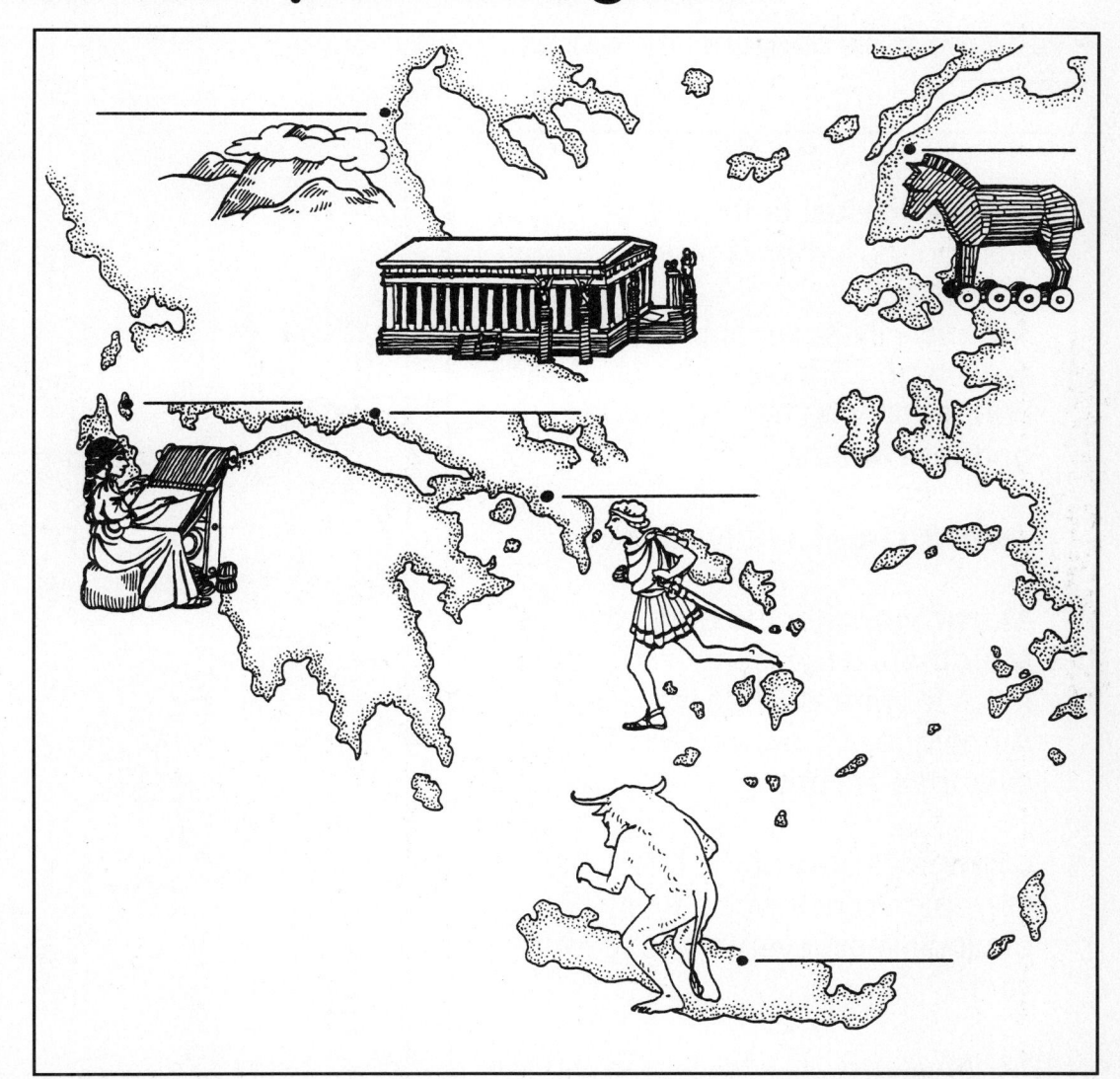

Name _____

Ancient Greece

The Greek world of myths and legends

The Greek world of myths and legends

♣ Read the clues and label the places on the map.

Troy: where the Greeks besieged the city for ten years and captured it from inside a wooden horse.

Knossos: home of the Minotaur.

Delphi: people came here to ask the god Apollo for advice.

Athens: Theseus arrived here with only one sandal.

Ithaca: where Penelope waited so patiently for Odysseus.

Mount Olympus: home of the gods and goddesses.

History

111

Ancient Greece

Name _____

Mapping the Ancient Greek world

Mapping the Ancient Greek world

♣ Read the clues and label the places on the map.

Helicarnassus: birthplace of Herodotus, father of history.

Athens: city-state, flourished in the 4th and 5th centuries BC. The Parthenon was a temple of the goddess Athene.

Sparta: a military city-state.

Marathon: after the battle of Marathon, a messenger ran ten miles to Athens to tell the Athenians of the Greek victory over the Persians.

Olympia: home of the first Olympic Games which were originally held every three or four years.

Name _____

Ancient Greece

A time-ribbon of key events

A time-ribbon of key events

♣ Place the following events along the time-ribbon. Use reference books to find out more about them.

- Homer writes the *Iliad* and the *Odyssey* (around 800BC).
- First Olympic Games held (776BC).
- Peloponnesian War between Athens and Sparta (431–404BC).
- Beginning of the Persian Wars (490BC). 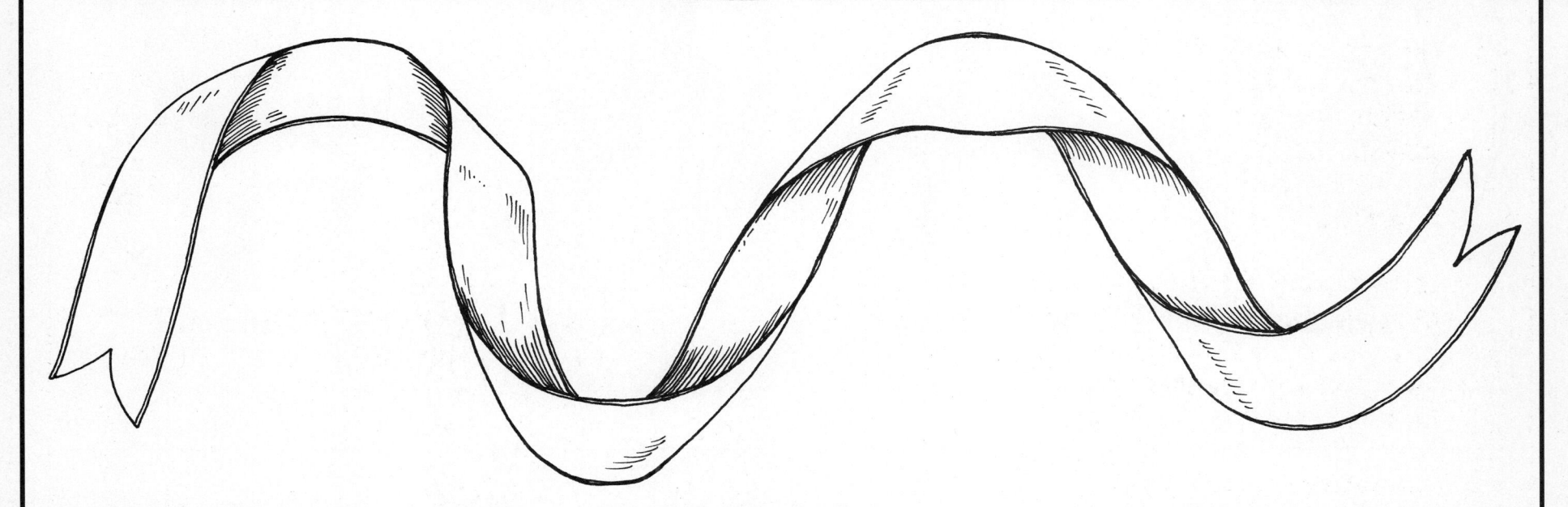
- Construction of the Parthenon in Athens begun (448BC).
- Alexander the Great conquers Persia and advances into India (327BC).
- Romans take control of Greece (146BC).
- Birth of Christ.

History

Ancient Greece

Famous Greeks

Name _____

Famous Greeks

✤ Find out more about these famous Greeks.

Homer 　　　　**Helen of Troy** 　　　　**Hippocrates** 　　　　**Herodotus**

_____　_____　_____　_____
_____　_____　_____　_____
_____　_____　_____　_____

✤ Using reference books, find two more famous Greeks. On the back of this page, draw pictures of them and write about why they are famous.

History

Name _____

Ancient Greece

The 1992 Olympic Games

The 1992 Olympic Games

♣ Using reference materials, provide the following information about the 1992 Olympic Games.

Place held	
Three types of events	
Three famous participants	
Prizes	
Clothes worn	
Length of time games lasted	
Any other information	

♣ Now use reference books to fill in the same information for the ancient Olympic Games.

History

Ancient Greece

Name _____

Vase paintings

Vase paintings

Paintings on vases can provide evidence about life in Ancient Greece.

♣ Use reference books or other source materials to find more evidence about daily life from vase paintings.
♣ Design your own vase decorations in the spaces provided.

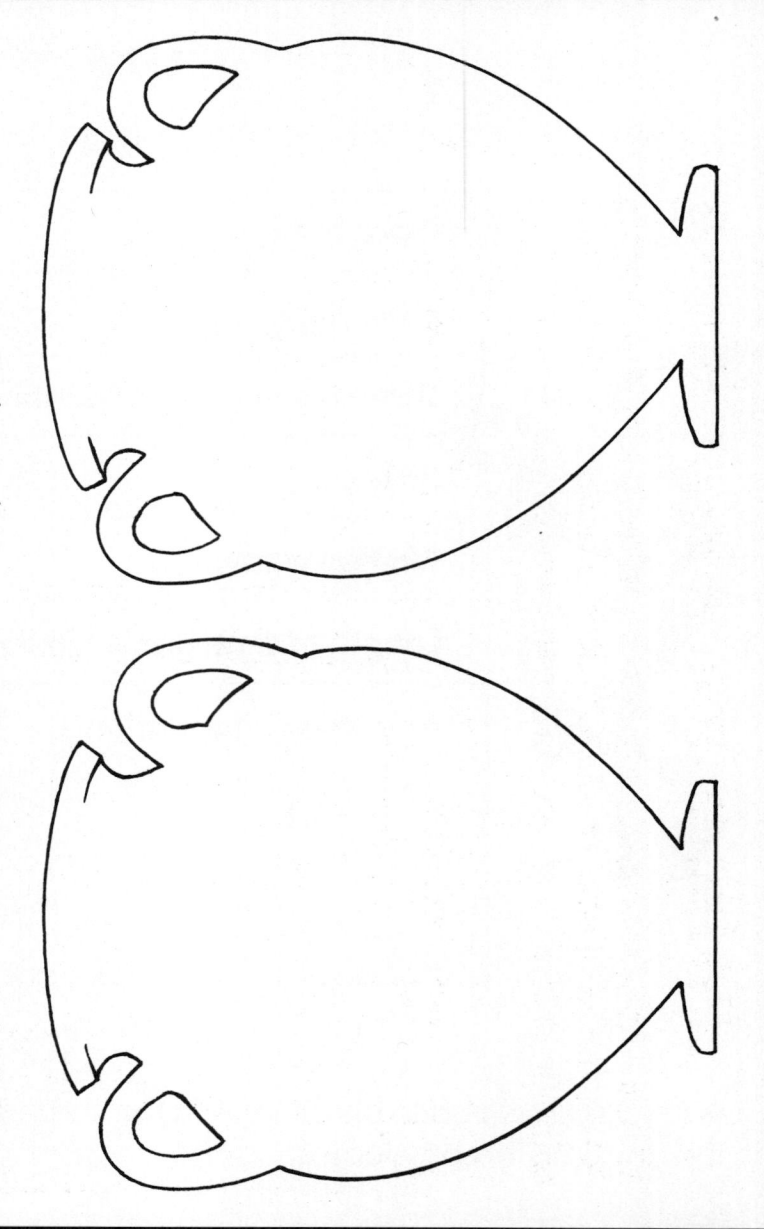

116

History

Name _____

Ancient Greece

Evidence from Ancient Greece

Evidence from Ancient Greece

Evidence about ancient history can be divided into four categories.
♣ Find out what each one means, then draw or write about one example of each from Ancient Greece. Record your source.

Literary

Source _____

Epigraphic

Source _____

Archaeological

Source _____

Numismatic

Source _____

History

117

Ancient Greece

Ships and shipping

Ships and shipping

This is a drawing of a trireme, which had three banks of oars and 170 rowers.

♣ Use reference books to find out more about the trireme and what it was mainly used for.

♣ In the space below, draw or write about other types of boats used by the Ancient Greeks.

♣ Discuss the differences and similarities between ships used in wars, ancient or modern, and those used to transport people and cargo.

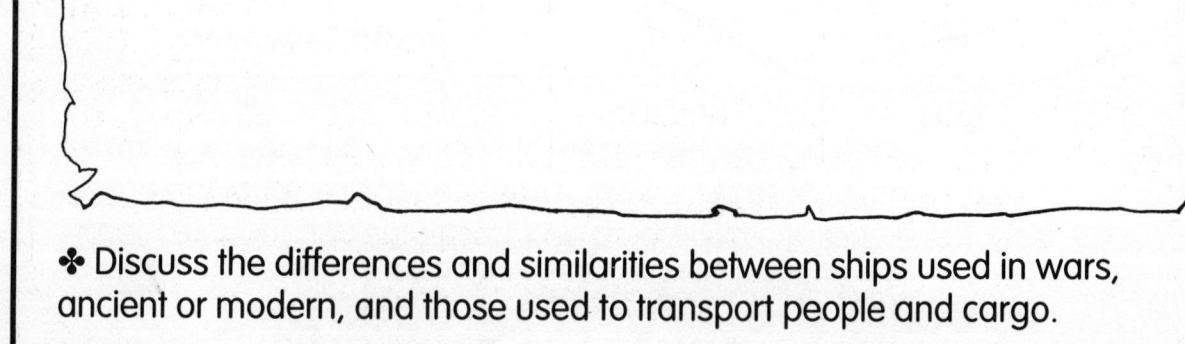

Name _____

Ancient Greece

The Greek alphabet

The Greek alphabet

Capital	Lower case	Name of letter	English sound
Α	α	alpha	a (l**a**d)
Β	β	beta	b (**b**in)
Γ	γ	gamma	g (**g**od)
Δ	δ	delta	d (**d**am)
Ε	ε	epsilon	e (l**e**t)
Ζ	ζ	zeta	z (**z**ebra)
Η	η	eta	e (**ai**r)
Θ	θ	theta	th (**th**istle)
Ι	ι	iota	i (**i**n)
Κ	κ	kappa	k (**k**ing)
Λ	λ	lambda	l (**l**id)
Μ	μ	mu	m (**m**et)
Ν	ν	nu	n (**n**ot)
Ξ	ξ	xi	x (la**x**)
Ο	ο	omicron	o (p**o**t)
Π	π	pi	p (**p**et)
Ρ	ρ	rho	r (**r**un)
Σ	σ/ς	sigma	s (**s**at)
Τ	τ	tau	t (**t**on)
Υ	υ	upsilon	u (f**ew**)
Φ	φ	phi	ph (**Ph**ilip)
Χ	χ	chi	ch (lo**ch**)
Ψ	ψ	psi	ps (**ps**eudo)
Ω	ω	omega	o (**aw**e)

❖ How many letters are there in the Roman alphabet that we use in Britain?

❖ Which of our letters are 'missing' from the Greek alphabet? Which letters do we not have?

❖ Write your name below using the Greek alphabet.

History

119

Ancient Greece

Name _____

Technology problem from Ancient Greece

Technology problem from Ancient Greece

✤ Can you help this Greek woman solve the problem? Remember:
- There was no tap at the bottom of an amphora.
- It was too big to lift and pour.

Use the following equipment to help you:
- large bottles filled with water
- plastic tubing
- cups

'How do I get the wine out without disturbing the sediment?'

In wine, the 'sediment' is the solid matter which settles down to the bottom.

120

History

Name _____

A past non-European society – the Aztecs

Planning grid

A PAST NON-EUROPEAN SOCIETY – THE AZTECS

KEY QUESTIONS	CONCEPTS	CONTENT	RESOURCES, TYPES OF SOURCES	ACTIVITIES, TEACHING AND LEARNING METHODS	RECORDING AND ASSESSMENT
• Where did the Aztecs live?	• Empire • Civilization • Trade and barter • Religion and rituals • Evidence	• Buildings • Appearance • Clothing • Family life • Food and farming • Trade and barter • Occupations • Crafts • Beliefs and rituals • Technology • Writing	• Reference books • Visual sources • Written accounts • Travel brochures • Large-scale map of Mexico • Museum visit	• Locating Aztec empire on maps • Group research into different aspects of Aztec life using range of resources and presentation styles • Using Aztec writing • Using Aztec designs in own drawings	• Can say where the Aztecs lived • Can select appropriate research sources • Ability to extract and transfer information • Can talk about aspects of Aztec life • Ability to explain the Aztec defeat • Show understanding of the range of issues involved
• What happened to the Aztecs? • What were the effects of exploration on the New World and the Old World?	• Conquest • Chronology • Conversion • Empire • Cause and consequence • Slavery • Conversion • Empire • Trade	• Cortés' campaign • Reasons for Aztec defeat: inferior weapons, belief in bad omens, poor leadership, impact of disease • Aztecs: new animals and technology brought in, land and gold taken, many enslaved, forced conversion, disease spread • Spain: expanded empire, new products and trade routes, increased wealth, power and prestige	• Reference books • Visual materials • Time-line • Maps • Reference books • Collection of foods from New World	• Teacher presentation on sequence of events • Group use of sources to draw pictures of key events on time-line • Finding clues to the Aztec defeat • Class discussion of moral aspects of campaign • Group research and discussion • Individual lists of good and bad effects on Old and New Worlds, giving own viewpoint	• Ability to identify some of the effects on the Old and New Worlds • Ability to offer and justify own viewpoint

History 121

A past non-European society – the Aztecs

Name _____

The world in 1450

The world in 1450

This map shows the world as it was known in 1450.
♣ Find Britain, Portugal, Italy and the African continent.

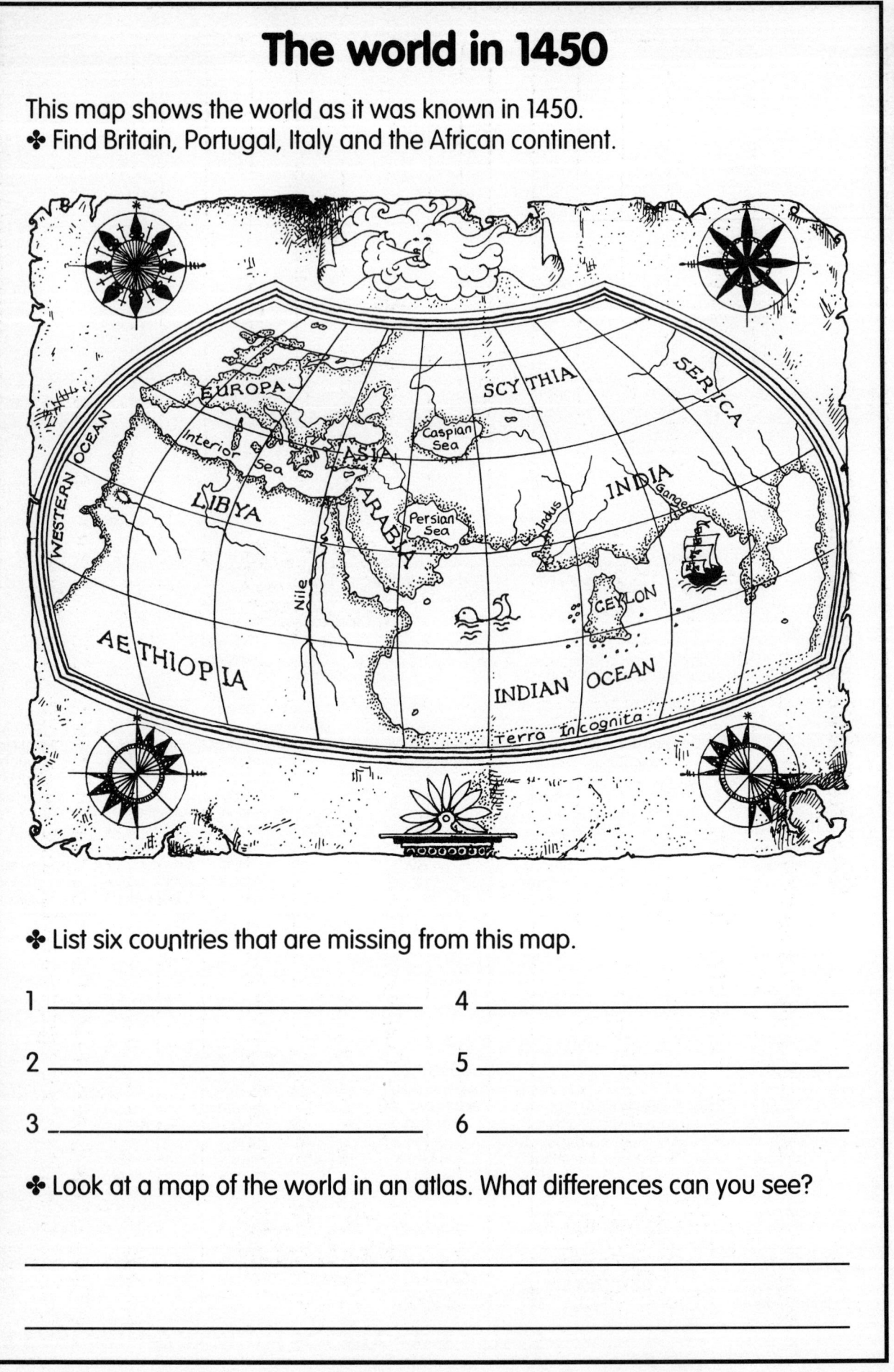

♣ List six countries that are missing from this map.

1 _____
2 _____
3 _____
4 _____
5 _____
6 _____

♣ Look at a map of the world in an atlas. What differences can you see?

_____
_____
_____
_____

122   History

Name _____

A past non-European society – the Aztecs

Exploration time-line

Exploration time-line

♣ Use reference books to find out about these famous explorers.

Name – **Ferdinand Magellan**
Date of journey _____
Destination _____
Other information _____
_____
_____

Name – **Vasco da Gama**
Date of journey _____
Destination _____
Other information _____
_____
_____

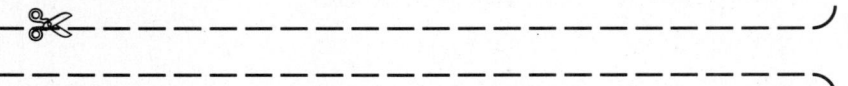

Name – **Christopher Columbus**
Date of journey _____
Destination _____
Other information _____
_____
_____

Name – **John Cabot**
Date of journey _____
Destination _____
Other information _____
_____
_____

♣ Draw a time-line. Write 1450 at the start and 1550 at the end. Cut out the pictures and put them in chronological order to make an exploration time-line.

History

123

A past non-European society – the Aztecs

Name _____

Columbus and his crew

Columbus and his crew

On 3 August 1492, Columbus set sail from Spain with three ships – the *Santa Maria*, the *Niña* and the *Pinta*. He hoped to sail west until he reached India.

♣ Find out whether he managed to reach India by sailing west.

Here is a list of some crew members on one ship.

The *Santa Maria*

Boatswain
Caulker
Ship's boy
Surgeon
Interpreter
Secretary
Royal Controller of Accounts
Marshal

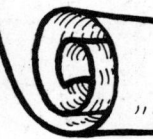

♣ Find out what work each one would have done.
♣ Why did Columbus need them on board?

124

History

Name _____

A past non-European society – the Aztecs

The Old World meets the New

The Old World meets the New

On 12 October 1492, Columbus reached land. He went ashore on an island which he named San Salvador, meaning 'the Holy Saviour'.
The people living on the island welcomed Columbus and his crew. These two illustrations show two versions of their first meeting.

♣ Look carefully at the pictures. On the back of this sheet, make a list of the things that are the same. Then make a list of the things that are different.

History

125

A past non-European society – the Aztecs

Name _____

Aztec life

Aztec life

This picture shows scenes from Aztec life.

♣ Look carefully at the picture and describe what is happening. What does the picture tell us about the Aztec people and their way of life?
♣ Find more information in reference books.

Name _____

A past non-European society – the Aztecs

Aztec men at work

Aztec men at work

This picture shows some of the work done by Aztec men.

♣ Look carefully at the picture. Describe what is happening. What information does the picture you give about the occupations shown?
♣ Why are there no women in this picture?
♣ Use reference books to find out about the role of women in Aztec society.

History

127

A past non-European society – the Aztecs

Name _____

Clues from the ground

Clues from the ground

Much of what we know about the Aztecs has come from the artefacts they left behind. These objects can give clues to what life was like at the time.

♣ Look carefully at the Aztec objects shown below. Answer the following questions, in the spaces provided, for each object.

1. What do you think it is? Give your reasons.
2. What was it used for?
3. Who might have used it?

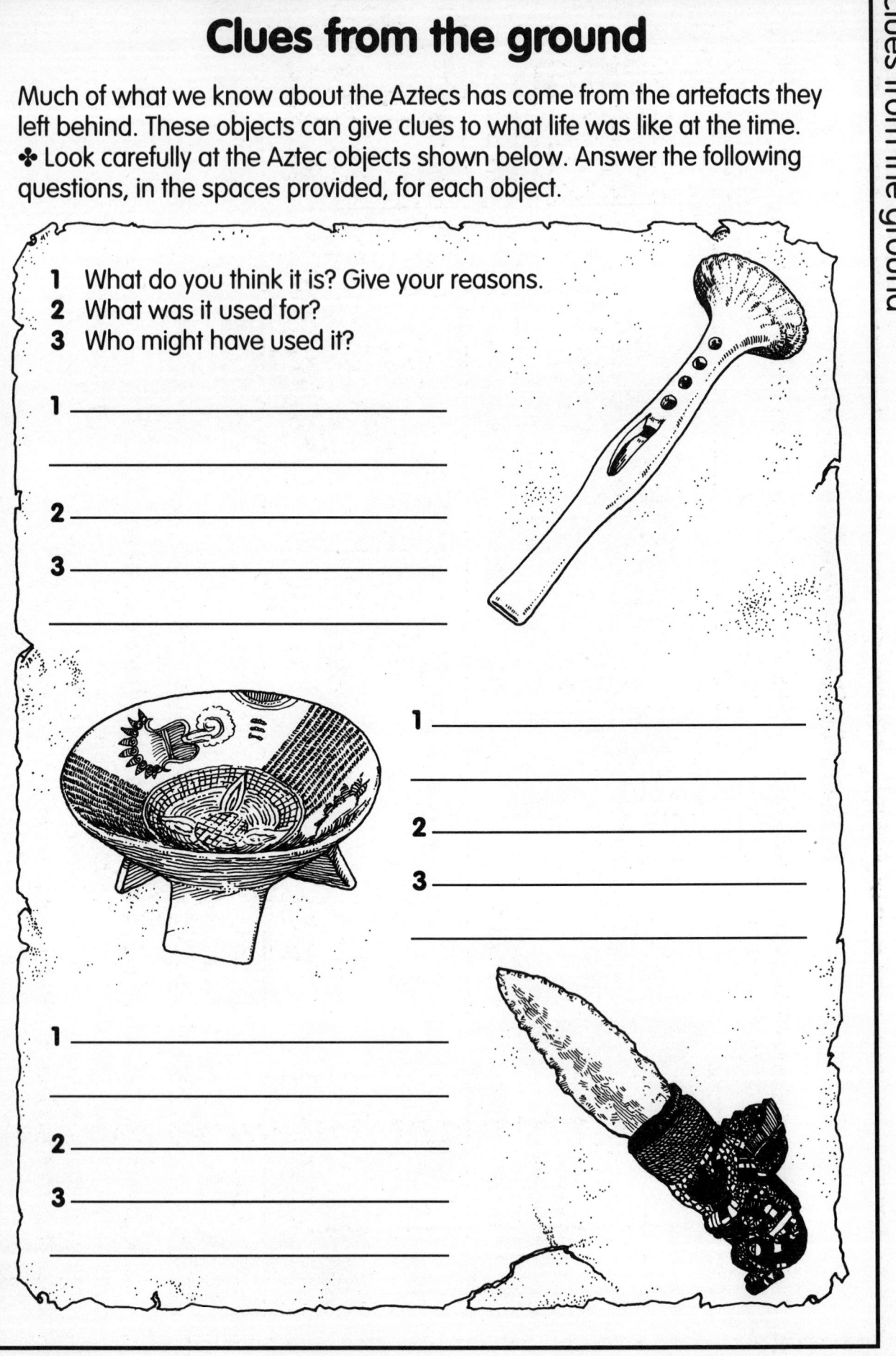

1 _____
2 _____
3 _____

1 _____
2 _____
3 _____

1 _____
2 _____
3 _____

128

History

Name _____

A past non-European society – the Aztecs

Aztec writing

Aztec writing

The Aztecs did not have writing as we know it today. They had no alphabet and used picture writing. These pictures are called 'glyphs'. Here are some examples.

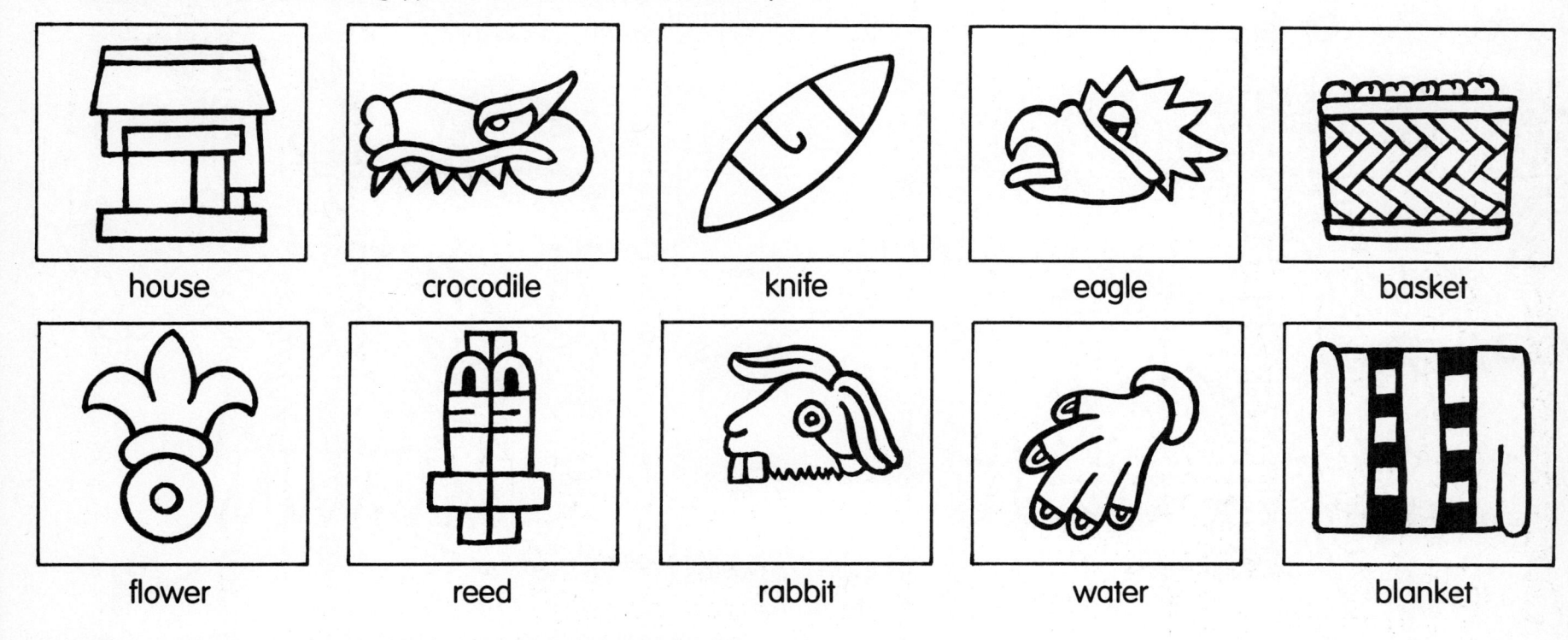

house	crocodile	knife	eagle	basket

flower	reed	rabbit	water	blanket

♣ On a separate sheet, design glyphs for the following words.

grass   lizard   head-dress   mask   child   corn   jar   temple

♣ What are the problems with this kind of writing?

History

129

A past non-European society – the Aztecs

Name _____

Aztec gods

Aztec gods

The Aztecs worshipped many different gods and goddesses. Here are images of two of them.

♣ Draw your own designs for two other Aztec gods. You can choose from this list:
- Tlaloc, the rain god;
- Xiuhtecuhtll, the fire god;
- Centeotl, the corn god;
- Xoltl, the monster god;
- Xochiquetzal, the flower goddess.

Quetzalcoatl, god of the morning star and of the rising sun

Mictecacihuatl, goddess of death

Name _____

A past non-European society – the Aztecs

The defeat of the Aztecs

The defeat of the Aztecs

The Spanish soldiers defeated the Aztec warriors in a very short time. These two illustrations show battles between the Spanish and the Aztecs.

♣ Tell the story of each picture. Find the clues that help to explain why the Aztecs were defeated. Make a list of these on the back of this page.

♣ What other reasons for the Aztec defeat can you think of? Reference books will help you here.

History

131

A past non-European society – the Aztecs

Name _____

The effects of exploration

The effects of exploration

The explorations and discoveries had important effects on the New World and the Old World. Some of these effects were good, some were bad.

❖ Discuss with your friends what you think the effects might have been and write about them in the spaces below.

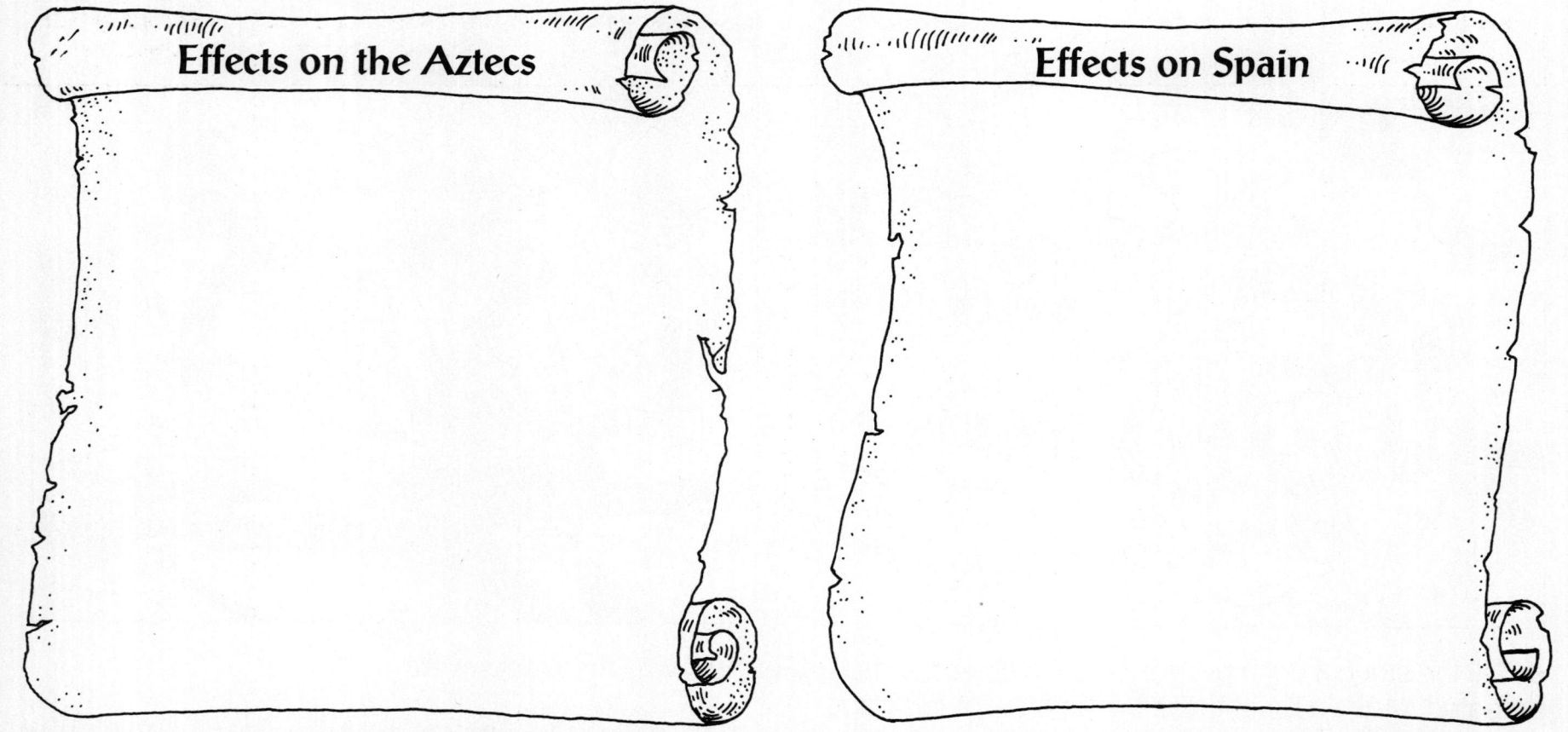

Effects on the Aztecs

Effects on Spain

❖ What do you think about the explorations? Were they a good thing or not? Give reasons for your point of view.

General

Teacher planning grid

Teacher planning grid

Teacher _____ Title of history unit _____

Year _____   _____

Class _____   Term _____

Key issues	Concepts	Content	Resources, types of sources	Activities, teaching and learning methods	Recording and assessment

General

Pupil record sheet

Pupil record sheet

Name _____   Title of history unit _____

Year _____   _____

Class _____   Term _____

Key issues examined	Historical concepts covered	Content	Resources, types of sources	Activities undertaken	Recording and assessment (including ATs and levels reached)

General

Resource evaluation: teacher's sheet (1)

Resource evaluation: teacher's sheet (1)

Study unit _____   Year _____

Details	Comments
Artefacts	
Visual	
Written	
People	
Suggestions	

General

Name _____

Resource evaluation: teacher's sheet (2)

Resource evaluation: teacher's sheet (2)

Study unit _____ / _____   Year _____

Details	Comments
Teacher's resource books	
Reference books (children's)	
Schools broadcasts/videos	
Visit	
Suggestions	

136

History

Name _____

General

Pupil ideas sheet

Pupil ideas sheet

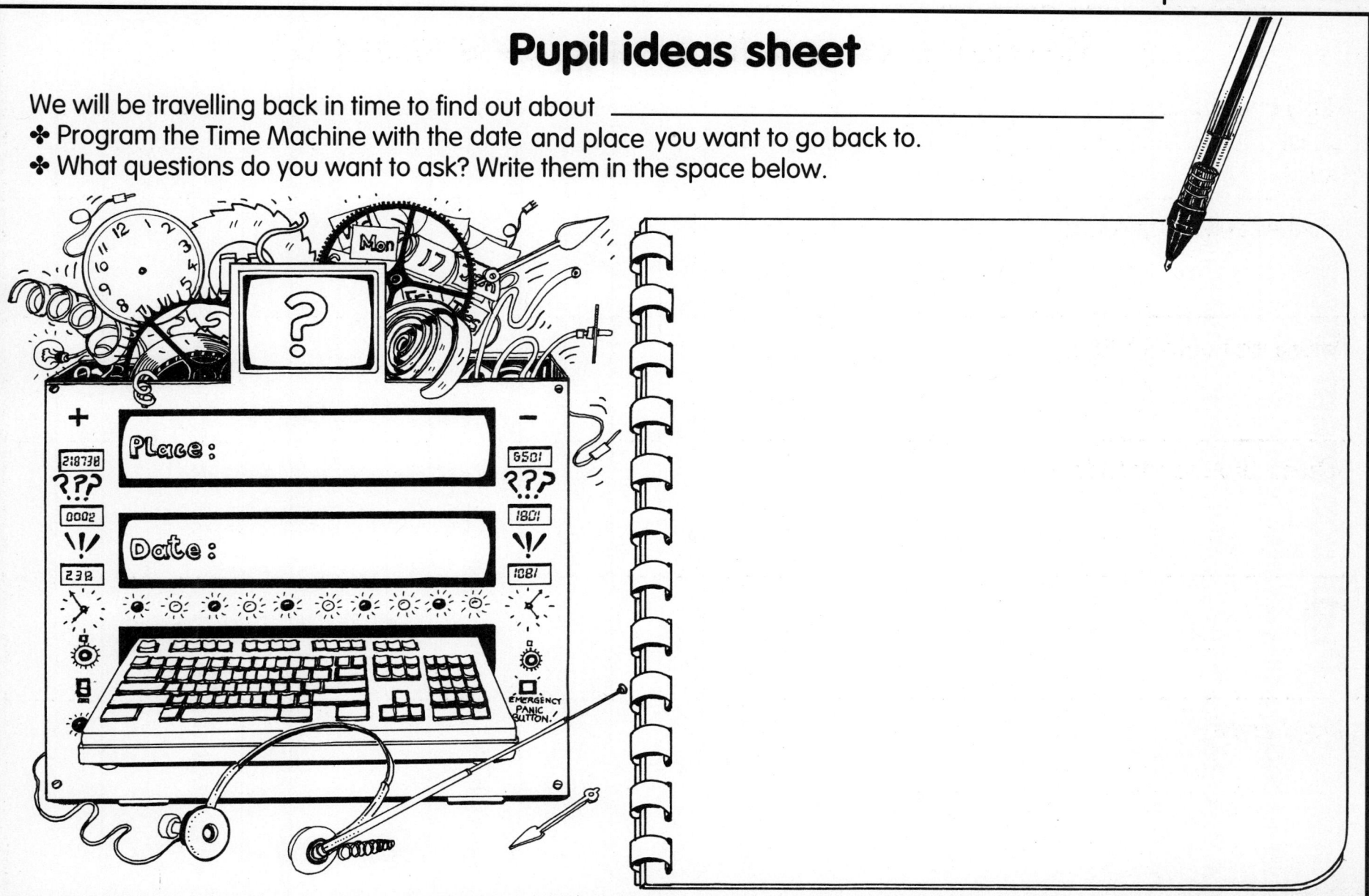

We will be travelling back in time to find out about _____
♣ Program the Time Machine with the date and place you want to go back to.
♣ What questions do you want to ask? Write them in the space below.

History

137

General

Name _____

Pupil comment sheet

Pupil comment sheet

You have been finding out about _____

♣ Think about all the work you have done and answer these questions.

What was the most interesting thing you learned? _____
_____

What did you enjoy the most? _____

Why? _____
_____

What did you enjoy the least? _____

Why? _____
_____

What surprised you the most? _____

Why? _____
_____

What would make this topic better for another class? _____
_____

History

Name _____

General

History detectives: using evidence

Historians find out about the past in different ways.

✤ Fill in the boxes to show how you found out about _____

We used:

Pictures

Artefacts

People

Written evidence

✤ What other evidence did you use? _____

✤ Which did you enjoy the most? _____

✤ Why? _____

General

Name _____

Investigating an artefact

Investigating an artefact

♣ Handle the artefact with care and answer the following questions.

What colour is it? _____

What shape is it? _____

What does it feel like? _____

What is it made from? _____

How old do you think it is? _____

Give your reasons: _____
_____
_____
_____

What do you think it is? _____

Who might have used or owned it? _____

How was it used? _____

Do you like it? _____

Give your reasons: _____
_____
_____

♣ Now draw a picture of the artefact on the back of this page.

General

Our class museum

Our class museum

Item number	Details
A picture of the artefact	Description _____ Measurements _____ Weight _____ Materials _____ Condition _____ Date _____ Origin _____ Other information _____

General

Time-line

Name _____

Time-line

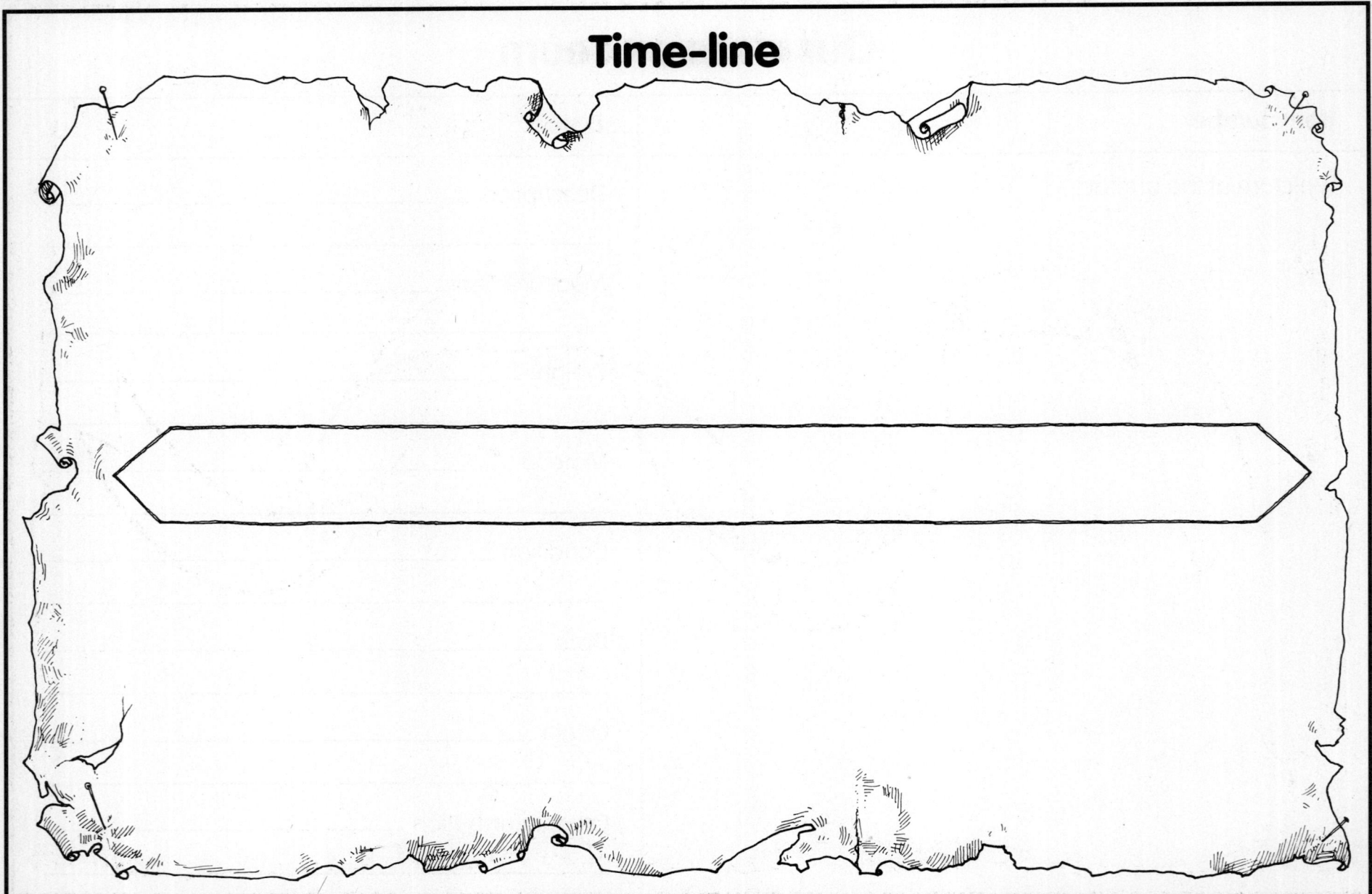

142

History

Name _____

General

Time-ribbon

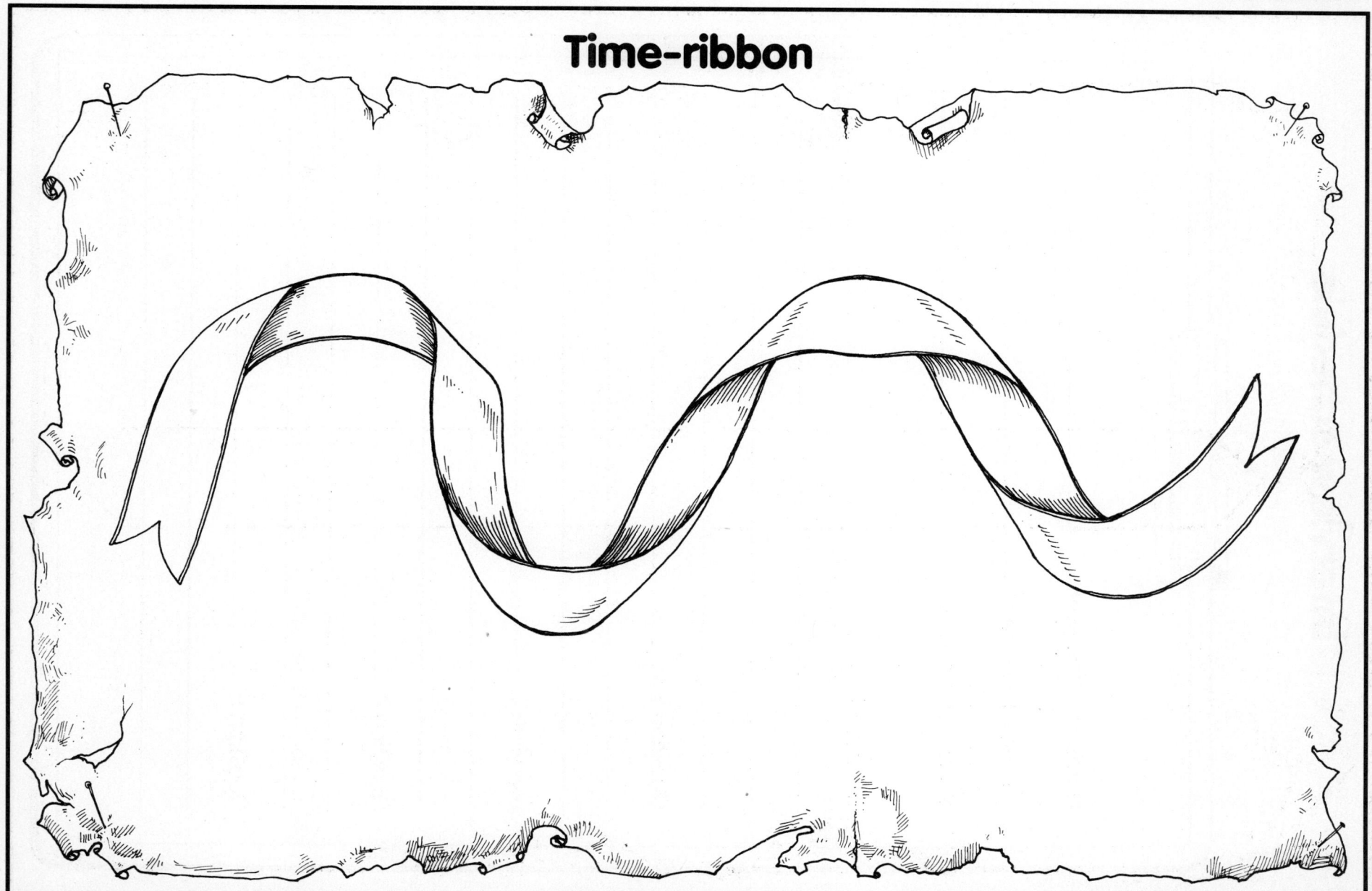

Time-ribbon

History

143

General

Interview schedule

Name _____

Interview schedule

Name of interviewer _____

Person interviewed _____

Subject of interview _____

Question 1 _____

Question 2 _____

Question 3 _____

Question 4 _____

Question 5 _____